THE HARDCORE
PREPPER'S GUIDE TO

SURVIVAL

BARTERING

LIVE WITHOUT DOLLARS
AND
LIVE WITHOUT DEBT

By David Presnell

www.SurviveUntilTheEndComes.com

THE HARDCORE PREPPER'S GUIDE TO

SURVIVAL BARTERING

LIVE WITHOUT DOLLARS
AND
LIVE WITHOUT DEBT

By David Presnell

ISBN-13: 978-1530198634

ISBN-10: 1530198631

www.SurviveUntilTheEndComes.com

Disclaimer

This publication is designed to provide accurate and authoritative information with regard to the subject matter covered. However, the author is not a doctor, lawyer, accountant, or other professional. Some of the material in this publication has been passed down to the author from generations, and some comes from the author's memory of his own experiences and research. Part of the material presented in this publication is of the author's own personal opinions or theories. People discussed in this publication may be fictitious to help present a point, idea, opinion, or theory. This publication is sold with the understanding that the author is not engaged in rendering medical, legal, financial, accounting, or other professional advice. If medical advice or treatment, financial services, or other expert assistance is required, the services of a competent professional person should be sought. This publication is sold with the understanding that the author cannot accept responsibility for any injuries, loss, or damage that may result from the use or misuse of following any of the text or information contained herein, nor be liable for legal prosecutions that may arise as a result of following any information contained in this book. The material provided herein is provided for informational and entertainment purposes only. If you should use any of the information in this book for any reason, you do so entirely at your own risk.

Trademarks

Any trademarks used in this book are the property of their respective owners.

Special Thanks

I would like to thank Almighty God for giving me the ability and ideas to create this book. Without God, this book would not exist. All power, glory, and honor go to God. I would like to thank my dear wife, Deborah. Without her excellent proofing abilities, her patience, and her motivation, I could never have made this work presentable to the public. I also want to thank Tiffany Crouse for her proofing and helpful suggestions in producing this book. I would also like to thank my many friends who have helped me, directly and indirectly, over the years, with ideas and helping me practice the methods mentioned in this book. I wish to thank my friend Steve Kuehn for his excellent input & suggestions for this book. Finally, I also want to thank you, the reader, for buying this book. Without you, there would be no need for me to have written it.

David Presnell
Author

Table of Contents

INTRODUCTION

When disaster strikes and takes out all forms of modern financial operations and banking systems, will your cash be worth anything? I don't think it will. Even if the dollar survives, there is a good chance that the prices on valuable commodities such as water, food, and safe shelter will skyrocket. If you don't believe it will happen, then consider what occurs every time a storm does severe damage to an area. Some people start selling gas for twice what it normally sells for and water for ten times what it sells for, so it does happen.

In this easy-to-use training guide, we will look at common sense real-world bartering for survival and the best things to use for bartering. You will learn what a good trade is and how to make the very best deal where everyone walks away happy. You will also learn how to deal with the thieves and rip-off artists who would steal your goods, and you will learn how to protect you and your goods with non-violent methods and with force if necessary.

There is also a special section in this guide that looks into the destructive aspects of using debt as money, and some secrets of getting out of debt fast and taking back the control of your money. You will also learn how to find money now and how to quickly build cash for the purchase of bartering items you will need soon, when all hell breaks loose.

This is a no nonsense – highly condensed easy-to-use training guide. I will not waste your time with 500 pages of technical reasons why you need this guide or how great it is. In just a few words from now, you will start learning how to barter. You will quickly master the twelve secrets to my way of bartering. I call them lessons. In fact, there are hundreds of lessons in this guide, but I only point out twelve.

Let's face it, the world is changing fast! World economic disaster looms, and if that's not enough, terrorism is expanding and world war seems to be just around the corner. Still in doubt? Record breaking natural disasters are happening almost daily. The internet is alive with dire warnings about swarms of earthquakes occurring around old volcanos which may be a sign the big eruption is near. We hear about record rain, record snow, record droughts, and other record-breaking weather events almost daily. World war seems to be lurking in the air. Wouldn't this be a good time for you to learn to barter & trade, before things collapse? Learning to trade & barter is a great skill that is both fun and rewarding even if disaster doesn't happen for a long time. Thank you for purchasing this book. A short time from now, I think you will be glad you did.

THE ART OF BARTERING

What is Bartering?

Bartering has been around since the beginning of time. Suppose you have something I want or need and I have something you want or need. If we're smart, we'll learn to trade with each other. I call that trading bartering. Of course, I could earn fiat money from a job or the sale of something and try to offer this in exchange for your goods and services. As long as the Government's idea of a good economy holds together, we may be able to continue for a long time trading this worthless paper for goods and services. In fact, many experts would tell us that a society cannot exist without government produced and backed exchange notes or money. They will also tell us that bartering would never work over time. With that said, I believe bartering has been around much longer than fiat currency. It seems to me that failure of governments and economies would prove the worthlessness of fiat currency over time. There seems to have always existed some form of money to fill in for bartering's gaps. For example, it would be difficult to swap a third of a living hog. So the person of the past might offer some form of money as change, or maybe some worthless paper with some fancy printing on it as a promise to give more meat later, when the hog is butchered, as part of the deal. These part barter, party money exchanges still go on today. You swap your old car in for a new one and give the dealer cash to pay for the rest of the cost of the new car. Your cash usually comes from a loan that you pay back over time. That, as you will learn, is a poor way of trading.

There has been all kinds of complicated mathematical formulas and theories to try and explain or understand bartering. None of that matters. What matters is that when you have a need, you will be able to exist or survive through your ability to negotiate a good trade or barter with someone else, without getting ripped off or killed. This skill of bartering will be extremely beneficial during hyperinflation or any other time that money may not be available. In fact, it's quite beneficial to know how to barter right now in 2016.

Can We Depend on the Government When Times Get Hard?

Consider the counterfeiting of fiat currency that goes on during wars to try and destabilize the opposing countries economy. Wars are costly. Guess what has historically boomed during wars? That's right, bartering. Most governments historically ban bartering during war, calling it the black market or other bad sounding things. They also ban the storage of food and supplies too. They call it hoarding. What a bad word. So, we are supposed to depend on a government, who has gotten us into war, to provide our water, food, clothing, shelter, and monetary needs. In history, the people of war-torn countries usually end up starving, hungry, and broke, with no help from governments. Of course, the United States of America would never do that to us, would they? That was over there. We have never really been truly invaded here in America and I hope it never happens, but if history is a clue, some country will probably try and invade us sooner or later. Why wouldn't they want to invade us? We seem to have everything "they" want, and it would seem we have lowered our defenses against attack.

Everything at one time or another has been traded or bartered, and it's been going on for a long time and it still goes on today. Bartering is not limited to goods. Bartering has been used for services as much, if not more than for goods. If you have a skill I need or desire and I have some material thing or a skill you need or desire, then the possibility for barter exists. The art of bartering comes from knowing how much each item, skill or service is worth in exchange. This is not a simple task. Many complex systems have been developed that try to give order to or control the process of bartering by setting exchange rates. Some try to make it like trading stocks or trading paper fiat money for work. I have read very complex technical books on bartering that get into advanced mathematics to try and figure out complex methods and exchange rates for bartering. They never work! Why? Because I might be willing to pay five times what someone else thinks something is worth as long as I can barter for it. It happens to be something I need and want very bad. That's called a free market system. That's just one reason. Bartering for food is very different than bartering for nails and a hammer. Bartering for nails and a hammer is very different than bartering for a small generator and twenty gallons of fuel. Things barter at different levels of desirability and perception of value for each different group of items based on needs or demands. That's another reason why complex bartering systems don't work. Skills and services barter totally different from things. If you have appendicitis bartering for a surgeon would be very different than bartering for an electrician to fix your generator. What about a generator that runs the surgeon's office? The electrician that repairs and maintains that generator could command much higher rates of barter than the surgeon could from his or her patients. That's another reason I call it an art.

Learning How to Barter – My Way

It can take many years of experience to develop the skills of knowing or *feeling* the value of exchange. This requires knowledge and a great amount of common sense. I have developed teaching methods that help people learn faster and I have incorporated those methods into this guide. This guide is based on many of the old-style bartering and trading methods mastered through years of actual trading experience of myself, my ancestors, and the many people I have traded with. Becoming skilled at bartering requires getting out and trading with people. You will make some goods trades and you will make some bad trades. You need to get burned a few times by making a few (hopefully inexpensive) bad trades for the valuable experience you will receive before your life depends on it for survival. The art of bartering can be learned faster using the practice lessons outlined later in this guide, and it's a lot of fun. Read and ponder this powerful guide a few times through. Then, start trading, swapping, dealing and bartering as much as you can now and you will develop the knack of bartering. Be honest and follow the proven principles in this guide. Quickly learn from your mistakes, correct your mistakes, and get back to bartering. You will start developing you own unique methods and ideas about value. Consider your trading and bartering sessions the classroom. Take your trades, both good and bad, with a smile and learn from the experiences. You will, in time, following this guide, become an expert at bartering.

THE SURVIVAL EVENT

Let's pretend that a survival event so devastating occurs that large numbers of the population die. Let's assume that banks and the stock market shut down, indefinitely, and electricity stops, indefinitely. Fuel stops flowing, and suddenly, the survivors become totally dependent upon their own resources. This happens quite regularly in war-torn third world countries. What's left of the government declares martial law and puts what is left of the military on active duty on American soil to protect us from ourselves. Let us hope and pray to God Almighty that such a day never comes.... but could it happen? You bet it could, and many things natural and man-made could cause it to happen. It's happened many times before in history and sooner or later a major world disaster will happen again right here in America. It's inevitable! Remember, humans have survived many more years without electricity that with it. In mankind's thousands or millions of years (depending who you ask), cell phones, computers, automobiles, microwaves, and electricity itself has only been available for a very short time. Everybody says, "technology is here to stay." Is it? We have become totally dependent on technology that can be wiped out, forever, by a simple magnetic wave from outer space. "Oh, that will never happen," some say. Well, solar storms hit the earth all the time. In history, some believe solar storms have hit the earth in the past that if occurred today, would take out electric grid down for a long time. It's just a matter of time until a real disaster happens.

The clock is ticking. The eruption of just one old major volcano here in the United States could take us back to the Stone Age in a few hours. The big biblical earthquake seems to be near. Nuclear war, terrorism, bird flu, new and deadly viruses, total world economic collapse, and of course something from outer space striking earth could all require us to become totally dependent upon ourselves for survival, possible for a long time. People often laugh when they hear about catastrophic events happening on earth. I just remind them about the dinosaurs. How

15

long did it take for the dinosaurs to become extinct? However, there is always hope. If I felt there would be no hope, I wouldn't waste my time writing this or any my other survival books. In fact, I'm a very positive thinker. Knowing how to survive is a positive skill. With God's help, humans have a powerful capacity and desire to survive, at all costs. Once the event has occurred, and some time has passed, I fully believe that humans will come back. It is in our nature to come back from disaster. If it be God's will, man will continue on. It is the time from when the disaster happens to the reestablishing of society that, I believe, we will be on our own. That period may be days, weeks, months, or years. Master bartering and you will have one valuable skill set to help you survive while others may not. Becoming skilled at bartering and trading will be very beneficial to you now, even if a major disaster doesn't happen in our lifetime.

What Would Happen to Money?

After such a major disaster occurs, would ink on paper be worth anything? No! The government would probably develop some kind of rationing program and fiat currency which would push inflation to well over a thousand percent. Current dollars or greenbacks might have a declared trade-in value or simply be declared worthless. You might be able to swap a current dollar for a thousand new coupons of fiat currency that you will use to make purchases with. Capitalism will abruptly end. During such an event, fiat currency, in my opinion would be worthless for the purchase of gold, silver, high quality food, and probably trade. They may be called rationing coupons, purchase stamps, or new world order dollars. It will not matter what they call the almost

16

worthless paper money. A can of beans that cost $1.00 before the event will be so high in price, most will not be able to purchase one, if any even becomes available. If the event is severe enough, governments and money may become non-existent.

In fact, would gold or silver be worth anything? I do not believe so. But so and so told us to "buy gold or silver for the hard days ahead." If you have gold and silver and I have meat and bread, no amount of your gold and silver will buy my meat and bread. On the other hand, if you have an extra 16-ounce canister full of propane and an extra propane stove and I have extra meat and bread, we can do business. Bartering goods and services will be the money of the day.

Here is your first lesson: I do not need a propane stove or extra canister full of propane. I have plenty on hand. But I know someone else who would swap five one pound packs of cured bacon for that small propane stove and canister of fuel. I know another person who happens to love bacon and has not had any since the disaster event occurred and he's sitting on a stockpile of ammo that's he's been saving up for years. I negotiate with him and he agrees to trade a 1,000 round box of 22 long-rifle bullets for four pounds of bacon. He considers it a great deal since he has thousands of rounds still on hand. I now break the box of bullets into small bags of 50 rounds each which I can trade for just about anything I want. Now, that's what I call bartering, all based on our theoretical disaster event, of course! Read this lesson again and be sure you fully understand its meaning before you move on.

What's It Worth?

How much will one item be worth compared to another item? First, it depends on the severity and length of the event. A two-week event such as hurricane or tornado will not create the need and demand for bartering that an event lasting many years would, such as world war three. After that, it is totally up to the individuals and how honest and fair each person involved in the barter is. If someone has a gun and decides to use it to secure food, they may kill me and take my meat and bread. My meat and bread just became worth the price of a little piece of lead and copper and a human life. How necessary is any item to human life? Who will you trust? I personally believe that before any real honest form of bartering can take place, most of the "I'll take it by force" type people will have to have destroyed themselves before those willing to work together will be able to. This would mean that you will probably have to quietly take care of yourself, and your family, in a very secret and protected place, maybe for several weeks or months, totally unnoticed, before you ever venture out and make your first real trade with decent people.

That is exactly what I believe must happen before bartering will become effective or available. You must be prepared to hide out and be totally invisible to those who would take what you have. If you think you have the firepower to defend you and your possessions, then sooner or later someone will come along with more firepower. Firepower can be a good thing if you are highly trained and experienced in its use. However, if they do not know you exist, then you will not have to fight them. If you carefully hide your barter possessions in many different places and make yourself unseen as discussed later in this guide, they may not consider you a person of any value. They may not even consider you a threat. They may not know you exist. The idea is to become "not worth robbing or killing." We will get into this in more detail later. Just remember that everything has a perceived worth or actual value to someone else and the value or worth is constantly changing and is different for each person and each trade.

Protecting Yourself

Will a time come that your very survival may require that you arm yourself for your own protection and to keep people from stealing your possessions? Probably! Could a time come during such a devastating event described above, that in order to protect you, your family, and your possessions, that you may have to kill or be killed? It's more likely than not. Are you prepared for that kind of head-to-head confrontation? Your possessions become your money. I know, people will tell me that nothing is worth dying for. That's very true in a normal world. But things change during disaster, especially disasters lasting for many years. Dying a slow painful death from starvation because thieves stole your food is a bad thing too. Whether we like it or not, or agree with it or not, it is very likely that food and fresh water will become "worth dying for" by many people during a major disaster event.

The Best Weapons

Your knowledge and skills, and ability to use both, become your weapons of warfare. Use your brain! Your brain is the best weapon you have, and that is lesson two. Train your brain and your body. If you do have hard weapons such as guns and knives, learn how to use them well and practice often. Learn how they work. Learn how to service and repair them. If you own firearms, learn how to clean them and load ammo for them. You don't have to set up a loading bench, but knowing how to load ammo may be of real value if times get hard. If you own knives, learn how to put a razor edge on them and learn – from an expert – how to knife fight or at least defend yourself from knife attacks. In my opinion, knives, in the right hands, can be much more effective than guns, especially when the attacker is within arm's reach.

When it comes time to barter items of great value, will two armed guards and a sniper on the roof be of value during the transaction? I would think so. What if you do not have a sniper and two armed guards working for you? You must think your way through to safely make the exchange. "I'm unarmed and alone. I have today's items of barter. You could kill me and take them or you could be sure I live to make it back another day. I have many more items carefully hidden in many various places away from where I live that will be very valuable to you and me, but only if you help keep me alive." Get the picture?

Have you ever noticed how many of the terrorists on TV wear masks to keep their identities hidden? During a real survival situation when bartering, it is vital for you to maintain strict secrecy about where you live and where your most valuable barter items are stored. Learn to pay attention to anyone that may be following you or watching you from a distance. You can always have secondary places with only a few minor items to advertise and learn how trustworthy your new barter friends are. If they have bad intentions, they will try to follow you and secretly or openly steal your items. Don't ever expose your hiding places to anyone!

The event has occurred. You have managed to collect some barter items as discussed later in this guide, and you have developed some highly tradable skills that will be worth a lot to many people as the event unfolds in time. Let's learn to barter.

LEARNING TO TRADE AND BARTER

Relative Value

Let's talk about relative value. A pound of real cured and smoked bacon is worth about $5.00 at this writing in a typical grocery store here in the southeastern United States. How much will this pound of real bacon be worth during the event described at the beginning of this guide? If you have been starving for days with only a few wild greens, that pound of high protein, high fat meat may be worth its weight in gold and maybe a lot more. If you are starving, fat meat provides more calories ounce per ounce than just about any other source. And it would also provide a high amount of protein. Relative value suggests that the pound of bacon is worth just about anything you are willing to give for it. How bad do you want it? How bad does the other person want what you have? Some people will refuse to eat bacon even if they are starving. It may be true that cured bacon with all the salt and preservatives may not be good for you, but neither is starvation. Case closed!

Equitable Trade

Relative value or perceived worth suggests that all the people involved in the trade must be happy with the trade or the trade isn't equitable. An equitable trade, in my opinion, is when both parties engaged in the barter are happy with the trade. Can you store sides of bacon as money? You will probably not be able to store them for too long. You can store a few one-pound cans of ham that will keep outside a refrigerator for a long time, maybe years. What will a one-pound can of ham be worth? If the other person has an excess of what you want or need, then you can receive a relatively high value for your ham.

Suppose you need fresh drinking water. The person who wants your ham has a sealed deep well with a solar-powered pump and an endless supply of fresh clean water. That person will likely swap many gallons of water for the ham, provided you have containers to put the water in. (Good containers will be worth their weight in gold, too.) On the other hand, if there are only ten gallons of fresh water left in town, you will be lucky to get a single swallow of water for that canned ham. If you trade your ham for ten gallons of water then you have established the relative value for each, at least at that exact moment in time. The value will change for the next trade of either. Your trade could have made the items future value or perceived value more or less valuable, depending on true availability.

See the point? If you have plenty of what they want and they have plenty of what you want, then equitable trade between the two of you should be a simple matter. If either side limits the quantities of the desired items by choice (a good idea for security reasons alone), or the items are truly scarce, then the relative value of the items goes up drastically, as it should. In bartering, there is no, such thing as price gouging. Some people will simply ask too much for what they have. If people trade with them at the price asked, then the items are apparently worth what they asked for them, at least to someone. And at that moment of agreement, that point in time that an offer of trade is accepted by both parties, a relative worth or value is established. That is lesson three: An item or service is worth exactly what someone else is willing to pay or swap for it. Read all this again. Be sure you understand this important valuable lesson. It is key to becoming a great trader, and it's far more powerful than simple supply and demand. It's psychology!

The Power of Desire

All relative values are based totally on availability and scarcity of the items or services offered and someone else's desire to have these items. Ponder that statement for a moment. The more people who desire to have these scarce items, the higher the perceived value. The items or services may not actually be scarce, but perceived to be scarce by most people who desire it. Perception mixed with strong desire or lack of desire can drive values up and down dramatically. Companies make millions of dollars creating the illusion that some new product is scarce, when in truth, millions of the item are in warehouses and in full production in factories. When desire is at the perfect high, the company releases a few to the market. They sell out quick, driving the perception of scarcity and prices even higher and get free national publicity at the same time. Remember that!

Your skills may be very valuable. If you were a highly-experienced vehicle mechanic before the disaster event, you will be able to barter those valuable skills after the event, as well. You may have to adapt, but things will have to be kept running such as generators and maybe an old truck that was made before electronic ignitions. If you were a surgeon before the event, you can be sure you will be able to barter your services for food and just about anything else you desire.

When Is a Trade Bad?

How will you know if the trade is equitable? If someone offers you a gallon of water for all you have, forget it. The gallon of water will not last you through the day. It's not worth it. They are trying to gouge you. The trade is not equitable. Find another source for your water. Remember, scarcity and availability is the key. Never let panic make your 'buy and sell' decisions for you. If someone gives all they have for that gallon of water, you can be sure that panic played a role. Smart thinking surely did not. An item traded out of panic or fear is not necessarily worth the price paid. Be calm and use great amounts of common sense.

Making Your Trading Safer and More Valuable

Lesson four: Don't present all your items at once. If you have

24 jars of peanut butter, present only one at a time and not very often thereafter. Each jar will become more valuable. If you come out with a case, you are not going to get as much for them and you could lose your entire case to robbers. If you keep the case hidden and present only one jar at a time only occasionally, you will make each trade safer, and as long as people do not know you have 23 more jars, you will force the value up over time. If you are the only one in the area that possess a quantity of items, keep it to yourself and keep them hidden. This is as true today as it will be in a disaster. Let go of one item just as if it is the only item of its kind left in the world. As long as no one else is offering these items for trade, the value will increase. Presenting one at a time will be much safer. Hide the items and hid their location.

Let us look at another way. You have an underground well and a pump that will deliver water to a tank inside your house. The power is off for a long time to come due to the emergency. You also have a generator that will power the pump to your well and you have enough fuel to run it an hour a day for several months. Your pump delivers ten gallons per hour. In one hour you can fill up three 35-gallon water containers. You have enough of these stackable containers to hold 350 gallons of fresh, clean drinking water. You also have hand pumps to transfer water to other smaller containers such as clean one-gallon milk jugs. If you tell the world you have an operating fresh water well, when no one else in the area does, there is a good chance the government or some thieves will take your well. In fact, you may not live very long after making it public that you have the only operating drinking water well in the area. So what do you do? Never tell anyone, and I mean anyone about your well, pump, or generator. Never run your generator when people may hear it running. Never trade water anywhere near the location of your well – your home. You must not let anyone know that you have water at your home or you will become a target. Fill one small one-gallon container with water and carry it to some location far away from it source and trade it there. It will command a good value. Get your jug back if you can. On your way home, make sure no one follows you home. You will eventually find trustworthy people to trade with, but never let them know you have more than one - anything. Carefully ponder all this now, before disaster strikes. And never present all your items at once.

A 28-ounce jar of peanut butter is worth about $5.00 today. What will it be worth during our survival event discussed at the beginning of this book? You can bet a large jar of peanut butter will be worth its weight in gold. I do believe it is better to have two small jars rather than one large jar. That applies to just about anything during a disaster. If you have two 16-ounce sealed jars of peanut butter or one large 28-ounce jar, I believe each of the smaller ones will be worth about the same relative value as the large one. And that is lesson five. Learn it well! Keep the large jar to eat, yourself, and barter smaller jars. If you put it another way, a five-gallon jug of fresh drinking water will have a certain relative value. Five one-gallon jugs of fresh drinking water presented for barter, one at a time, at different times, may be worth almost five times more than the one jug of five gallons. The jugs themselves have high value, too. This all works because people have come to expect discounts for quantity purchases. A half-gallon of name brand milk at the grocery store costs as much or more than a gallon of the store brand. And the store brand is usually just as good. The reason people pay the high price for the half-gallons is that they just do not need a gallon. This will apply during a disaster but in reverse. When someone is thirsty and in need of water, they will see only water. One gallon or five gallons will make little difference to them provided that have limited items to barter for the water. Now if they are in the trading business and have water, your one gallon will not be worth as much.

Consider another example. A four-pack of AA batteries may have about the same barter value as a twelve-pack. People will simply see it as a pack of batteries. Present three four-packs to barter at separate times and you may receive three times the barter value that the one twelve-pack would have received. Quantity discounts will probably not apply in a system of bartering except with those who try to make a living off of bartering and trading itself. You might even be able to barter good AA batteries one or two at a time, depending on the needs of the other person.

It's About Perceived Value

Someone who has plenty of gasoline might offer you a gallon of gas for a pack of AA batteries. Another person might offer you a pound of ham for a pack of AA batteries. Someone else might offer you a box of .22-caliber long rifle ammo for a pack of AA batteries. A four-pack of AA batteries will be of value since four batteries will run most devices; however, a twelve-pack will not be perceived at a much greater value. You will probably be offered the same gallon of gas for the twelve-pack. On the other hand, a two-pack of AA batteries may have a low barter value because two batteries will not run many devices except a small flashlight. Having small shortwave radios that run on two batteries will be more tradable for the same reason. I have several really great shortwave radios that will fit in a shirt pocket and run on two AA batteries. What if you have four new rechargeable AA batteries and a solar battery charger that actually charges the batteries? The real value of your four rechargeable batteries and charger just went through the roof.

Inflated Value

Inflated value suggests someone is asking a lot more than something is worth. Think of the item's real value to you or someone else you know that may be interested in it. How long will it last? Is what you are trading more valuable than what they are trading from a desirability point of view? In other words, how many people desire what you have to barter? The more people who desire what you have, the better. Bartering is not that difficult. You have something somebody wants or needs. They have something you want or need. Maybe both of you are fair and honest people. An equitable trade should be quite simple. Bartering can include items and services, so don't forget your skills and knowledge. A good knowledge of first aid and survival can be of real barter value. A good set of skills in just about any specialty may be of value to you. If the value seems inflated, be patient. The worth of the item or service (its true cost), will drop when someone else presents the same item or service for trade at a lower offer.

Money, Gold & Silver

So what may constitute money in a survival situation as described at the beginning of this book? I have already stated my theories about the value of paper money, gold and silver. I should also say that there is nothing wrong with collecting some extra gold or silver, at least as a hobby. It will probably not be worth anything during the survival event, but the event may end someday and gold and silver may return as the financial standard. Cash will most likely be replaced with something (probably a chip implant), and we may become a cashless society. As far as having cash or gold and silver to buy things during the event, I wouldn't plan on it buying much, and I would never swap your valuable barter items for gold, silver, or cash. You could receive a truckload of gold, silver, and cash for five gallons of kerosene and you would not receive near enough for it.

Peoples Needs

When thinking about what may be valuable during an indefinite survival event, consider what things are consumed daily and where they come from. Remember, survival minded people will adapt. They might just stop drinking colas. Stocking a basement full of colas for hard times might not be such a great idea. A case of dated canned hams will be of good value. Before I get into specific items, be sure to date all the items you acquire for barter, including containers of water and fuel. You should use up items before their dates expire and replace them with fresh ones. It is easy to shelve or store items you use and keep a monthly check on the dates. Most food items have "best by" dates on the package. Most canned items in traditional sealed cans will last for years, but it is generally recommended to use canned food within a year. I'm not sure how long the new plastic pop-top containers will last. If you have a choice, choose metal sealed cans and sealed glass jars and stock some good quality hand operated can openers.

What will people need when the power goes out and traditional paper money becomes worthless? They will need water, food, shelter, and protection from many forms of harm. What items may constitute a barter value during such an event? Let's consider the size, first. You must be able to transport the items. Finding water will be of little long-term value unless you have safe containers to store it in. Finding a 500-gallon underground tank of fuel will be useless unless you can get it out of the tank and have containers to transport it in. Will fuel and water containers be of value? You bet. Will portable water and fuel pumps be of value? You know they will! To understand what might be of potential value, we must try to place our minds into those yet-to-happen survival events. We must find empathy for the survivors of such an event.

To practice just turn the power off for an hour or two during a busy time at your house. Don't leave it off long enough to damage the food in your refrigerator or freezer. Just long enough to practice and consider how it will feel if it never comes back on. Do the same with the water occasionally. It will be tough when it happens but it seems more likely than not that the day will come soon that we may be without many things we take for granted. This is a great way to test your survival supplies and equipment too. Learn what works and what needs improvement before disaster strikes.

WHAT TO BARTER

Fuel

The most likely item of barter value would be any form of fuel. This could be gasoline, kerosene, propane, butane, diesel fuel, pump-stove fuel, fuel oil, wood for fires and cooking, coal, charcoal, canned fuel, oil & fat, candles, and candle wax. All of these items would have a relatively high barter value early in the event. The problem with liquid fuel is, quite simply, long-term storage. Having a supply of gasoline or other flammable liquids on hand can be very dangerous and most liquid fuels deteriorate quite rapidly with age. Adding stabilizers to fuel and carefully monitoring the age of the fuel would be a necessity. Use up and replace any stored stabilized liquid fuel within a year.

One fuel item that may be very useful for barter is the small 16-ounce propane cylinders that you can buy at almost any camping store. These small propane bottles wouldn't be worth much, initially, but I believe as people use up their resources these propane bottles would become more and more valuable especially for people who are traveling by foot. Some of these 16-ounce cylinders are refillable. Having the ability to refill them from larger tanks would be of great value at least for a while. If you have full 20-pound propane cylinders, I would suggest you hide them and keep these for your own needs. These 20-pound cylinders are the kind that fit under your gas grill.

Another fuel related item that will be of high value and easily transported is a hurricane candle. These are the round candles designed to burn for many hours that are sold in the camping section. You can usually find them in dollar stores, too. They sometimes come in bags or packs of three. Open a bag and add a disposable butane lighter that works, a small box of strike-on-the-box matches, and a cheap aluminum holder designed for the hurricane candles. Seal the bag up and wrap a six-foot piece of duct tape around the bag. These little kits will be great items to barter. You can put ten of them on your bartering shelf for about $20. Even if you don't barter them, they will be of use to you, too. The duct tape has many uses and adds value to your little fire starting kit. You can also use tea light candles, available ten to a pack for about a dollar.

Other things that would be almost as valuable as fuel itself are things related to the fuel. The first things to consider are containers. Fuel containers of all types will become more and more valuable. Think about it. Everybody with a lawnmower has at least one plastic or metal gasoline container. What if 100,000 people suddenly needed to transport liquid fuel from one place to another? The containers would become almost as valuable as the fuel itself. Most big box, auto parts stores, and hardware stores have a few. They would disappear quickly.

Rotating Stored Fuel

The process of using up old items before they become too old and replacing them with fresh items for additional storage is usually called rotating the stock. Do not ever store fuel in the building you live in. It must be stored outside, away from any dwelling place, in a building properly prepared for flammable liquids. Another problem with fuel is the space it takes. Storing 500 gallons of liquid fuel would almost certainly require a special storage tank. Enough firewood to get you through one cold, powerless winter would require a large storage space. Now, we're discussing things you can trade for other things. If you have fuel and firewood, you would be wise to carefully hide them and only barter what you will not need. Even if you are using the fuel, it would be wise to barter it before it becomes too old to use.

Containers

Five-gallon (or six-gallon), fuel containers can be purchased for about $7.00 each. Never drink water stored in a fuel container and never put fuel in a container marked for drinking water. That could kill you. Green or blue plastic containers are available just for drinking water and are clearly marked for water. I know someone who placed many high-quality, five-gallon containers filled with water in his attic. The warm water acted as a passive solar heater in the winter and helped dissipate heat in the summer. With the addition of a fan system to move the heated air where needed, this system helped reduce his winter heating bill. When the power went out, he brought one of the containers down and poured it in the back of his toilet when he was ready to flush.

Some of the cheaper light blue and green containers will develop small leaks after about five years of treated water storage. The dark blue heaver cube shape water containers I use have never leaked. They are stackable and very high quality. I have never had any problem storing stabilized fuel in the high quality six-gallon red plastic containers. It pays to buy quality, especially for your own use.

How much will fuel containers be worth? It depends on how bad another person needs them. If fuel becomes available at a local gas station with a generator, you better have something to store and transport the fuel in if you want some of it. All the money in the world will not be worth anything if you do not have a safe container to carry that fuel in. Gasoline containers, kerosene containers, diesel containers, water containers, and propane cylinders with transfer adaptors will all be of great value during any survival event.

Accessories

Consider the things that are used up as the fuel burns. Wicks for lanterns and stoves, mantles for lanterns, wicks for candles, parts and supplies for common stoves and heaters, oil, filters, parts specially-designed for fuel-powered generators, and light bulbs. Think about accessories to the items that burn the fuel, such as drop cords for generators. A generator will not be worth much if you cannot get the electricity into the place where you need it. You will also need pots and pans for the cook stove, a solar battery charger for the automobile or a generator battery, and matches or lighters to start the fuel burning. Oh, don't forget the potential value of a fully-charged fire extinguisher. All these inexperienced people playing with fire and fuel will surely make fire extinguishers valuable. I'm sure you can think of other things that may become valuable. When you do write it down, maybe somewhere in this guide.

Electricity

Electricity will become a rare commodity during an event, such as the one described at the beginning of this book. Electricity may only be available to those who have a generator and fuel to run it, but don't plan on living like you do now. Other forms of electricity can be produced by batteries and solar panels. Some areas may have limited electricity on the power lines depending on the nature of the disaster and the damage to the power grids. If you happen to be one of the lucky ones who still has electricity, it probably will not stay on for long. Make valuable use of it while you can. Store as much water and fuel as you can and use or preserve the food in the freezer before your power goes out too. Can or cure the food from the freezer as soon as possible after the power goes out. Learn how to preserve foods the old ways. Get a good pressure canner and learn how to use it over a wood fire or propane burner. Be sure your heat source can heat the pressure cooker to properly can meat, typically 15 pounds' pressure for an hour or more. Practice with it until you are comfortable using the canned meat you produced on a wood fire, wood stove, or propane stove. Learn how to salt cure & smoke meat and dry fruits and vegetables properly now, before the power goes out for good.

Lights

A few 12-volt light bulbs with holders and wires will be of high barter value. You can find versions in the automotive electrical sections or make your own for under a dollar each. In fact, stocking an entire 12 volt wiring and bulb kit could be worth its weight in gold. The ability to string up a few lights and power them with a small solar panel or a small rechargeable battery will be of value. The solar panel can be one of the battery maintainers/chargers that sell for around $15.00 at automotive sections in big box stores. You can also purchase a few of the cheap solar LED yard lights and disassemble them to reuse for other uses. They come with a rechargeable battery too.

Batteries

In a widespread major disaster, it is likely that resources and skilled people necessary to keep the power plant generators running will be very limited. In an event such as an earthquake, it is likely that the electricity and other utilities, such as natural gas, may be turned off to affected areas for safety reasons. Batteries will be good for bartering for at least awhile. Batteries will eventually run down, so it is only a matter of time before they're all used up.

I would probably keep any batteries for yourself that run radios or other information equipment, as well as batteries for your flashlights. Rechargeable batteries and a way to charge them, such as solar, will be too high in value to barter. You should keep these for your own use. Some of the new AAA, AA, C, D, and 9-volt rechargeable batteries can be recharged up to 1000 times before becoming useless. Some of these batteries have a good charged shelf life and some will hold a full charge for only a few days.

Chargers for these batteries are available that can be used in a cigarette lighter of a car. Such chargers could possibly be converted to work from solar panels. Having the ability to charge these batteries for people would be of high barter value, but your methods and apparatus would have to be carefully hidden and protected because there would be some people who would try and take it away from you.

Radios

A small AM or AM/FM pocket radio, which you can find for around $8.00, may be a good barter item. Add a set of fresh batteries with it and its value will increase. At nighttime, an AM radio will pick up signals from hundreds of miles away. This will likely be a better choice for information than local FM radio. Small, inexpensive shortwave radios that fit in a shirt pocket and run on two AA batteries may be highly valuable for barter provided any signal exists for people to listen too. It is likely there will be some transmissions unless the entire electronic world has been fried with a catastrophic solar storm or massive EMP strike. Your large main shelter or home based shortwave radio (and extra batteries for it), will be much too valuable to barter. Keep it for your own use, and be sure you have plenty of batteries for it on hand.

Small Solar Panels

If you have solar panels or a wind-driven generator installed in your home, you may find them desired by others. America chose 120-volt alternating current or AC for its electrical needs early in the development of electricity. A few people believed 12-volt direct current or DC would have been more efficient, however it does not travel efficiently over long distances. This is the electricity your automobile supplies to run the lights and radio. Your 12-volt DC voltage can easily be run through a coil and stepped up enough to provide a high voltage for the spark plugs that run the engine in most automobiles. Solar electricity (without storage batteries), will be more usable if maintained and regulated to 12-volts DC. It doesn't take much of a solar panel to light a small 12-volt bulb, but the bulb goes dark when daylight stops hitting the solar panel. Small solar panels for under $20.00 that you see sold as battery maintainers may make good barter items, but don't depend on these cheap solar panels to provide dependable electricity for survival needs.

Power Inverters

This is a good time to bring up power inverters. These are the small boxes available in various wattages that you plug into a cigarette lighter or hook to your car's electrical system in some way. They change or convert the 12-volt electricity from your car battery into a form of 120-volt AC electricity. Power inverters usually have one or two regular three-prong sockets that you can plug a TV, radio, or computer into. Be sure and follow the manufacturer's instructions. If your car is not running, you will run down your battery, quickly. If your car is running and not moving, you will be wasting valuable gasoline.

Small, inexpensive power inverters that you can buy in the automotive section of your favorite department store may become highly-prized as barter items, at least until the gasoline is all gone. These same inverters can be connected to anything that produces

12-volt direct current, such as a correctly wired series of solar panels or a homemade alternator based windmill. To make the inverter work properly from solar panels or wind power, you must have a good storage battery system that produces enough amperage to run the inverter and any 120 AC devices attached to it. Once the batteries drop below the operating voltage of the inverter, the inverter will have to be shut down and the batteries allowed to be charged from the solar panels or windmill.

The instructions that come with good solar panels and inverters will explain all this in detail and you should follow them, carefully. You can purchase high quality solar & wind generator kits that come with storage batteries, regulators, and even backup generators depending on how much money you want to invest. You can research building your own backyard windmill on the internet. Remember solar panels on your roof, a windmill sitting in your back yard, or a running generator is a big target for potential thieves. You wouldn't be bartering your windmill or generator. You would be bartering the charging of batteries for people. You should be equipped to charge everything from small AAA up to large auto and marine batteries, such as the ones used with power generation systems.

Wire

Top-quality solar panels and storage batteries, if you have them, will be far too valuable to barter. However, 25- or 50-yard rolls of stranded 18-gauge wire designed for 12-volt DC applications in red and black may be valuable for bartering. Household 120-volt AC sheathed 14/2 wire with ground, or sheathed 12/2 wire with ground, in 25-foot rolls may be valuable for bartering. Black plastic rolls of electrical tape and screw-on wire connectors for 12-gauge, 14-gauge, and 18-gauge wire may be of barter value. Rolls of 100-foot copper wire are often used for shortwave antennas. These are sold as shortwave antenna kits with instructions for a few dollars in most electronics hobby stores. These should be of value since many people will try to increase their radio reception distance.

Novelties

There are several novelty items available such as hand-crank or squeeze flashlights and hand-crank radios. I would not place much survival value on these, but they may be of barter value and they are not very expensive. Some of the better ones let you charge up an internal battery but most do not run long until the cranking or squeezing has to be started again. Another item I think may be of barter value regarding electricity is the small inexpensive digital volt/ohm meters. You can buy these for a few dollars. You should also get a good one for yourself and keep it. The better ones sell for under $20.00. The small ones seem to work just as well and sell for around $5.00 at some electronics stores. A volt meter will be of great value to anyone trying to build an electricity generator, such as a wind-powered, water-powered, or solar generating device. Some mechanically-inclined individuals will likely try and use automotive alternators and generators to produce electricity. They may need to use a volt meter to help them with the task.

Food & Water

Food and water will be valuable, but should you consider bartering your supply? I personally believe you should carefully hide and guard your valuable food and water supply. If you have good food and fresh water, there are some people out there that just may want to try and take it away from you. If they do not know you have it, then they cannot take it, can they? If you have a clean running source of water such as a gravity fed spring (or a deep well with a pump that works), that you can hide and control, you could bottle and barter water (in small jugs over a period of time as discussed earlier). The problem would be keeping people from knowing your water location. Large groups may come and try to take your source away from you. Properly managed and protected, such a spring or well would allow the right person to become very powerful. Yes, there's a warning in that statement. Power and greed can lead to corruption. Entire communities could be created around such a spring especially if no other clean water exist in the area. Something to think about.

Water Purification

So, what may be good for barter related to food and water? Water purifying items will be highly-prized during a major disaster. Commercial water purifying tablets and kits can be purchased at sporting goods stores for a few dollars. Be sure to have some in your survival kit for your own use, too. Hand held pump or gravity water filters will be highly valuable for barter.

Small bottles of pure bleach (non-scented), that contains sodium hypochlorite and no other ingredients may be valuable as a water purifier and may have a good barter value. The old way to purify water (and still a good one), was to strain all particles from it through a paper or cloth filter, such as cheesecloth or coffee filter. Then, boil it for five to twelve minutes or five minutes plus two additional minutes for each 1,000 feet you are above sea level. If boiling was not possible, water could be purified by filtering and adding eight to twelve drops of pure sodium hypochlorite bleach per gallon of filtered water. The amount was doubled to 16-24 drops of bleach per gallon if the water was cloudy. Pure bleach, in small bottles, should have barter value, especially as water supplies deteriorate in quantity and quality. Remember, there may be little electricity to pump fresh water from the ground. Paper coffee filters will aid people who wish to strain their water, removing as many particles from the water as possible, thus these filters should have barter value too.

Ready-To-Eat Food, Junk Food, Drink, & Accessories

Anything related to food may be of potential barter value. Small cans of potted meat and Vienna sausages will always have a high barter value. Consider salt, pepper, and other seasonings; sealed, fresh, dated bottled seasonings such as hot sauce, steak sauce, mustard, catsup, soy sauce, and others; canned shortening and bottled oils for cooking; utensils commonly used in outdoor grilling such as tongs, spatulas, and fire resistant mitts; metal pots, pans, spoons and forks; plastic and paper plates, spoons and forks; rolls of paper towels; knives for carving, including old-fashioned inexpensive wooden handle butcher knives; small whetstones for sharpening, strike anywhere kitchen matches if you can find them, strike-on-the-box kitchen matches; and my favorite, toothpicks.

If you do not believe toothpicks are of value, just put a box in your pocket and start offering them to your friends, occasionally, during the day. You will be amazed at how many people will take them. There is a strange association between eating and good old toothpicks. They may not have a high barter value, but passing a few around during a survival event will probably not make you any enemies. Chewing gum and most junk food will have a relatively high barter value, as will tobacco products and anything with drinkable alcohol in it. These items provide no real survival value, and I would recommend that you do not swap your valuable survival food, water, or anything else for junk food, drinks, or smokes. However, if you happen to stock up on stick chewing gum, a few fresh dated, hard chocolate bars, a few cartons of name brand cigarettes, you may find them worth their weight in gold during a survival event. Should I mention the value of a few dozen small bottles of liquor? The size they serve on planes and in some hotel rooms would be perfect for barter. I guess they could be called single-serving size. I suppose having a few fifths of cheap bartering liquor on hand would be worth a lot in trade too, as well as a few fifths (or liters), of high quality name brand drinking liquors – for your own medicinal use of course.

There arc many other potential junk food items that may have a high barter value, but be sure the items have a long shelf life or "best by" date and rotate them with fresh items before the dates run out. Simply use the items now that are getting close to the "best by" date. Spoiled items or out-of-date items will be of little value. I have eaten many properly stored canned foods that's date was over four years past the "best by" date. I do not suggest eating out-of-date foods, but they may still be good. Dispose of swollen, rusty, or leaking cans of food, even if the date is still good. When you open a can of out-of-date food be sure it smells and looks good. If it has darkened or has any off odor, dispose of it. Cooking at full boil for no less than 25 minutes should kill off any bad bacteria.

Don't Consume Your Bartering Supplies

There's another problem most people don't think about when storing items like liquor and junk food in your house. There is a chance you will get depressed one day, break into your stash, and consume them before the disaster strikes. Odds are you are not going to break into your storage area to get a box of salt or a box of toothpicks. Thieves would never steal your stash of toothpicks and salt, but you can be sure they will take your ammo, guns and liquor. Think about that for a moment.

Pumps

I suggest you acquire two electric pumps, a 12-volt and a 120-volt, to move drinking water if the need ever arises. These small heavy-duty pumps are about the size of a shoe box and are designed to move several gallons a minute. One plugs into a standard 120-volt outlet. It will run well on a large gasoline powered generator. The other clips onto a 12-volt DC car battery or plugs into the cigarette lighter. Pumps, such as these, can be found for under $50.00 at many farm supply and hardware stores.

I believe you can also purchase these pumps from most mail-order tool catalogs. Some of these mail-order companies offer everything from generators to work clothes. Many of these firms offer solar electric kits and alternate heating units. The quality of most of the well-known mail-order firms has been high. Having the ability to pump water would possibly be of high barter value during a disaster. The pumps themselves would have to be kept hidden or carefully protected. If someone has transportation to a fresh water supply and you have pumps and containers, then the possibility for an equitable barter exchange exists.

Personal Items

Some personal items will be of high barter value. How about some stick underarm deodorant in both men's and women's versions? A good supply of firm toothbrushes may be of value. I suggest firm because they may last longer and they will be valuable for much more than just tooth brushing. Toothpaste might be of barter value. Small bottles of mouthwash may be tradable. The sealed boxes or packages of ready-to-use wet towels will be desirable but they do dry out after a few months of storage. Rotate them to keep fresh ones in storage.

Bars of soap will be valuable. Solar showers like you buy in the camping sections may be highly desired, but be sure you have one or two good quality ones for yourself. Razors of the disposable double-blade type for both men and women will be worth their weight in gold, as will small cans of aftershave and aftershave lotion. Let's face it! We, Americans, have become soft. We love to feel fresh and smell good. Our skin must be soft and our fingernails trimmed. Ah, a dozen pair of good quality fingernail clippers and toenail clippers will be highly tradable. Small pocket-size lotions may be of value. Fresh, dated, sealed medicine cabinet items such as eye drops, headache pills, cold pills, lip balm, and similar items may be of trade value.

Since I'm talking about personal items, can you imagine what a case of sealed tampons would be worth when women run out? What about cloth or disposable baby diapers? Baby powder in the small containers and ointment for diaper rash may be of value. What about glass baby bottle kits? What about fresh, dated, canned baby formula? What about rolls of toilet paper? All sizes of the plastic Ziplock® bags would be of high barter value. Can you think of anymore? These are all things that become money when paper money becomes worthless.

BARTER ITEMS LIST

This list is for your consideration only. It is not exclusive and it is certainly not exhaustive. I am sure you could think of many other great items that would serve as survival bartering items. You should not go out and buy any of the items on this list until you consider the best-by dates and storage space required. In addition, would you be able to use the items if time passes and nothing happens? Think about any purchase you make as an investment. How much could you get for each item if you had to sell them for cash? This will motivate you to look for bargains. As you go over this list, you will notice that it is in no specific order. That will help you think about other things as you read the list. When you think of something, write it down, maybe in the back of this book. You might circle the items that you believe would be most valuable to you.

[ ] Water Containers. Be sure the containers or jugs are sturdy enough to be reused

[ ] Non-Perishable Food

[ ] Heavy-duty plastic plates, spoons, forks, knives

[ ] Plastic food storage bags of several sizes

[ ] MRE's and freeze-dried meals

[ ] Heavy-Duty Nylon Reinforced Tarps.

[ ] 25-Foot Packs of 3/8-Inch Polypropylene or Nylon Cord

[ ] 25 - 50 Foot Lengths of Heavy-Duty 1" Polypropylene Rope

[ ] Rolls of Six-Mil Heavy-Duty Plastic Sheeting.

[ ] Family-Size and Two-Person Tents

[ ] Sleeping Bags of Various Sizes and Cold Ratings

[ ] Wool Blankets

[ ] Rain Suits Made of Vinyl or Rubber Including Pants full-length coat with hood

[ ] Disposable Biological / Chemical Suit (like used in hospitals)

[ ] Heavy-Duty, Long Gauntlet-Style Rubber Gloves

[ ] Heavy-Duty, Slip-On, Rubber or Vinyl Boots

[ ] Solar Showers (5-Gallon)

[ ] N95 Disposable Filter Masks

[ ] Full-Face Military-Style Gas or P100 Chemical Masks

[ ] Hard Hats with Winter Liners and Face Shields

[ ] Waterproof High Quality Rolls of Mil Spec Duct Tape

[ ] Spare Clothes and Shoes

[ ] Knives of All Shapes and Sizes

[ ] Sharpening Stones and Tools

[ ] Multi-Tools

[ ] Fire-Starting Kits

[ ] Strike-Anywhere Wooden Matches (sealed in plastic bags)

[ ] Disposable Butane Lighters

[ ] Magnesium Fire Starters

[ ] Fire-Starting Sticks

[ ] Zippo®-style Fluid and Flint Type Cigarette Lighters

[ ] Cans of Lighter Fluid for Zippo®-style Cigarette Lighters

[ ] Packs of Flints for the Zippo®-style Cigarette Lighters

[ ] Cooking Kits or Mess Kits

[ ] Pots and Pan

[ ] Coffeepots with well-fitting lid and fireproof handles

[ ] Fireplace Cooking Utensils, Forks, Tongs, Turners, and

Gloves

[ ] One-Burner and Two-Burner Propane Stoves.

[ ] Multi-Fuel Pump

[ ] Small Propane Cylinders

[ ] Salt, Pepper, Sugar, Spices

[ ] Hand Operated Can Openers

[ ] Bottle Openers

[ ] Dishwashing Liquid and Cloths

[ ] Scouring Pads

[ ] Cans Ajax® Type Powder Cleanser.

[ ] Fishing Kits

[ ] Zebco® 33 (or equivalent) Rods & Reels

[ ] Fishing Line in Various Test Weights, Fish Hooks, Sinkers, Snap Swivels

[ ] Traps and Snares

[ ] Snare and Trip Wire

[ ] Portable Battery-Powered AM/FM Radios

[ ] Portable Shortwave Radios

[ ] All Sizes of Fresh Alkaline Batteries

[ ] All Sizes of Rechargeable Batteries

[ ] Portable Battery-Powered Weather Radios

[ ] Programmable Hand-Held Police Scanners

[ ] Solar AAA through D Battery Chargers

[ ] 12 Volt AAA through D Battery Chargers

[ ] Flashlights

[ ] Propane Dual Mantle Lanterns

[ ] Extra Packs of Mantles for Common Lanterns

[ ] Pump-Up Multi-Fuel Lanterns

[ ] Old-style Kerosene Lanterns with Wicks are

[ ] 1-Gallon Factory Sealed Cans of Lantern Fuel, Coleman®
    Fuel, or Kerosene

[ ] Spare Parts for Pump Lanterns

[ ] Portable Propane or Kerosene Heaters

[ ] Candles

[ ] Reading Glasses (various powers up to 3.25)

[ ] Portable Chemical Toilets and Extra Chemicals

[ ] Personal Sanitation and Hygiene Items

[ ] Toilet Paper

[ ] Facial Tissue

[ ] Sealed Containers of Moist Wipes

[ ] Paper Towels

[ ] Feminine Hygiene Products

[ ] Tampons

[ ] Sanitary Pads

[ ] Underarm Deodorants

[ ] Aftershave Lotions

[ ] Body Powders and Sprays

[ ] Disposable Dual-Blade Safety Razors

[ ] Bars of Antibacterial Soap

[ ] Talcum Powder

[ ] Petroleum Jelly

[ ] Toothbrushes

[ ] Toothpaste

[ ] Small Sealed Bottle of Mouthwash

[ ] Washcloths

[ ] Hand Towels

[ ] Large Bath Towels

[ ] Plastic Pails or 2-Gallon Bucket with Lids

[ ] Plastic Cups

[ ] Don't Forget the Little Ones and the Elderly

[ ] Canned Baby Formulas

[ ] Diapers

[ ] Diaper Rash Creams

[ ] Baby Bottles

[ ] Children's Toys

[ ] Pacifiers

[ ] Contact Lens Solutions.

[ ] Hearing Aid Batteries

[ ] Denture Cleaning Solutions

[ ] Survival Rifles

[ ] Pistols

[ ] .22 Caliber Ammo

[ ] 9mm Pistol Ammo

[ ] .45 caliber Pistol Ammo

[ ] .223 Mil-Spec Rem Ammo

[ ] .308 Mil-Spec Ammo

[ ] Hunting Bows

[ ] Arrows

[ ] Crossbows

[ ] Bolts for Crossbows

[ ] Signaling Devices (whistles, flare guns, signal flares, signaling mirrors, etc.)

[ ] Bottles or Packs of Potassium Iodide Tablets (65mg or 130mg)

[ ] Binoculars

[ ] Tripod-mounted Long Range Spotting Scopes with Range Finders

[ ] Protective Devices and Equipment (fighting knives, clubs, pepper spray, Tasers)

[ ] Fire Extinguishers

[ ] Firefighting Equipment

[ ] Firefighting Protective Clothing

[ ] Radiation Detectors

[ ] Gas & Carbon Dioxide Detectors

[ ] Burglar Alarms

[ ] U.S. 1964 and Earlier 90% Silver Coins

[ ] U.S. 90% Gold Coins (NCG or PCGS Certified)

[ ] Digging and Trenching Tools

[ ] Folding Military-Style Shovels and Picks

[ ] Full-Size Round Point Shovels

[ ] Old-Style Mattock or Pick-Style Digging Tools

[ ] Cutting Tools

[ ] Bow Saws (with metal and wood cutting blades)

[ ] Woodsman-Style Single-Bit Axes

[ ] Chainsaws (each with a gallon of stabilized fuel mix & chain oil)

[ ] 6" – 8" Folding Saws

[ ] Generators & Stabilized Fuel

[ ] Quarts of 30 Weight Motor Oil for Small Engines

[ ] Non-Battery Operated Plug-in, Touchtone Telephones

[ ] Compass and Topographical Maps (of the general area you live in)

[ ] Waterproof Compasses

[ ] Windup Watches with Day and Date

[ ] Rolls of Piano Wire

[ ] Rolls 18- or 20-Gauge Tie Wire

[ ] Rolls of Twist Tie Wire

[ ] Rolls of 12, 14 & 18-Gauge Electrical Wire

[ ] Drop Cords of Different Lengths

[ ] Notebooks, Pens, Pencils and Sharpeners

[ ] Survival Manuals

[ ] Repair Kits

[ ] Scissors

[ ] Tweezers

[ ] Duct Tape

[ ] Electrical Tape

[ ] Filament Tape

[ ] Pliers

[ ] Wire-Cutting Pliers

[ ] Phillips and Flat-Head Screwdrivers

[ ] Rolls of Nylon 20-Pound Test Fishing Line

[ ] 72–Inch Shoestrings

[ ] Small Cheap Knifes

[ ] Safety Pins of Various Sizes

[ ] 500-Foot Rolls of Nylon Bricklayer's Line

[ ] Tire Repair Kits for Tube and Tubeless Tires

[ ] Plumbing Repair Kit with Assorted Washers & Screws

[ ] Tubes of Super Glue

[ ] Bottles of Contact Cement

[ ] Tubes of Silicone Adhesive

[ ] Sewing Kits for Both Clothing and Heavy-Duty Sewing, such as Canvas

[ ] Regular Sewing Thread

[ ] Darning Thread

[ ] Regular and Heavy-Duty Needles

[ ] Variety of Buttons

[ ] Small Backpack Style Mess Kits

[ ] Vehicle Fire Extinguishers

[ ] Jumper Cables

[ ] Small Tool Sets (including sockets designed for automobiles)

[ ] Plug Type Vehicle Tire Repair kits

[ ] Cans of Tire Sealer/Inflator

[ ] 12-Volt Portable Air Compressors

[ ] Tire Gauges

[ ] Heavy Work Gloves

[ ] Road Flares

[ ] Small Fuel Containers (empty) and Siphoning Hoses

[ ] Power Inverters 12-Volt

[ ] Backpacks

[ ] Duffel Bags

[ ] Drinking Water in 20-oz Plastic Bottles

[ ] Portable Backpack-Style Water Filters

[ ] Personal or Travel First Aid Kits

[ ] 10' x 12' Waterproof Lightweight Nylon Reinforced Tarps

[ ] Trash Bags (all sizes)

[ ] Rolls of 550 Military Para-Cord

[ ] Small Pocket-Size, Foil-Type Survival

[ ] Ponchos

[ ] Multi-Tools

[ ] Small High-Quality Backpack-Style Cooking Kits

[ ] Small Butane or One-Burner Propane Stoves

[ ] Small Manual Can Opener

[ ] Bottle Openers

[ ] Rolls of Aluminum Foil

[ ] EMP Protected Electronic Communications Equipment and Batteries

[ ] Packs of the Small Portable Toilet Paper Rolls

[ ] Containers Sunblock (SPF 30 or Higher)

[ ] Containers of Insect Repellent

[ ] Light Sticks

[ ] Small Personal First Aid Kits

[ ] Home and Auto First Aid Kits

[ ] First Aid Supplies

[ ] Canvas Triangular Bandages

[ ] 4" Self-Adhering White Sterile Gauze Rolls

[ ] 3" Self-Adhering White Sterile Gauze Rolls

[ ] 4" x 4" Sterile Gauze Pads

[ ] 3" x 3" Sterile Gauze Pads

[ ] 3" x 3" Sterile Gauze Non-Stick Pads

[ ] Large Eye Patches

[ ] Large Butterfly Closure Strips

[ ] Wound Closure Strips

[ ] Extra Large Peel-and-Stick Bandages

[ ] Rolls 1/2" Medical Tape

[ ] Rolls 1" Medical Tape

[ ] Rolls 2" or 3" Sports Tape

[ ] Rolls 2" or 3" Sports Foam

[ ] Rolls of Heavy-Duty Plastic Stretch Wrap

[ ] Splint Wire

[ ] 6" ACE® or Equivalent Stretch Roll Bandages

[ ] 4" ACE® or Equivalent Stretch Roll Bandages

[ ] Trauma Dressings

[ ] Pairs of Sterile Disposable Gloves

[ ] Emergency Blankets

[ ] Pairs High Quality Surgical Hemostats

[ ] Pairs of 6" High Quality, Medical Paramedic-Style

Scissors

[ ] Pairs of High Quality Medical Tweezers

[ ] Medical Quality Sterile Scalpels

[ ] Medical Quality Sterile Suture Kits (fine and medium)

[ ] Rolls of Heavy-Duty Dental Floss

[ ] Stainless Steel Dental Probe Sets

[ ] Small Handheld Non-Breakable Mirrors (about the size of a playing card)

[ ] OB Kits

[ ] Bottles of Sterile Eyewash with Eyecups

[ ] Bottles of Original and Moisture Restoring Eye Drops

[ ] Small Boxes of Cotton-Tipped Ear Swabs

[ ] Extractor Snakebite Kits (Made by Sawyer® and others)

[ ] Penlights

[ ] Oral Thermometers

[ ] Ice Packs (be careful not to crush them in the case)

[ ] Hot Packs

[ ] Bottles of Aspirin-Based Painkiller and Fever Reducer

[ ] Bottles of Naproxen-Based Painkiller and Fever Reducer

[ ] Bottles of Acetaminophen-Based Painkiller and Fever Reducer

[ ] Bottles of Ibuprofen-Based Painkiller and Fever Reducer

[ ] Single Use Packets of Aspirin (check expiration dates)

[ ] Single Use Packets of Naproxen (check expiration dates)

[ ] Single Use Packets of Acetaminophen (check expiration dates)

[ ] Single Use Packets of Ibuprofen (check expiration dates)

[ ] Bottles Anti-Diarrheal Liquid (extra strength)

[ ] Bottles Pepto Bismol™

[ ] Single Use Packets of Anti-Diarrheal Pills

[ ] Single Use Packets of Pepto Bismol™

[ ] Packs of Acid Reducer such as Tums®, Rolaids®, or Maalox®

[ ] Boxes of Non-Drowsy Formula Sinus Pills

[ ] Boxes of Antihistamines for Sinus

[ ] Boxes of Benadryl®

[ ] Boxes and Bottles of Laxative Pills

[ ] Bottles or Packs of Potassium Iodide Tablets (65mg or 130mg)

[ ] 8-oz Bottles of Betadine® Solution Antiseptic (Povidone-Iodine 10%)

[ ] 1-oz Tubes of Betadine® Ointment Maximum (Povidone-Iodine 10%)

[ ] 1-oz Tubes Triple Antibiotic Ointment

[ ] 1-oz Tubes Cortisone Cream

[ ] Tubes of Sunblock (SPF 30 or higher)

[ ] Bottles of Good Quality Insect Repellent

[ ] Bottles of Burn Cream

[ ] Solar Showers (5-Gallon)

[ ] First Aid Manual and Professional First Aid Training

Keep your supplies updated and clean. Replace items as used or if dates expire. Learn how to use everything in storage and rotate often. All these items don't have to be stored as a unit. They could be stored around the house and used as needed. In the event of an emergency, they can be pulled together to be more accessible. You may already have many of these items in your house. It would be a good idea to identify them and make a list, so you would have ready access to them when disaster strikes.

PROTECTING YOUR ASSETS

Hobo Life

To survive over the long-term, some of us may have to become like hobos. We may have to learn to accept our situations and make the best of what we have or can rake and scrape up. We may have to beg, borrow, and some may resort to stealing, but I don't recommend you do it. There will be those who will try to kill anyone who tries to steal what they have. Protect your assets by learning to carefully hide them. That's why people use banks. They think they can protect their money by hiding it in a bank, the safest place they know. Does anybody really know how safe banks really are? Do you know people who brag about how much they have? If they truly have what they claim, then they are begging some thief to try and take it away by boasting about it. It amazes me how people will announce on social medial (to the whole world) that their entire family is leaving town for a two-week beach trip. Then when they return, they just cannot understand why their house was robbed. Keep your wealth, your survival supplies, and your plans to yourself! Do not make it easy for thieves to break in and steal what you have! If people think you are penniless, then no one will try to rob you, will they? You just won't be worth the trouble. That can also work if people thing you are dangerous. In their mind, it would be far riskier to rob or attack you than an easier mark. Just a thought.

If a man put on a $10,000 suit, stuffed his hip pocket with a fat wallet, and walked through a high-crime district of any city, he would probably be robbed, if not murdered. If, however, he wore ragged pieces of clothing from a dumpster, wreaked of wine and body odor, and walked through that same high-crime neighborhood with empty pockets, there's a chance someone just might give him some money, especially if he asked. Better to look like a hobo (or at least fit in), in bad times than someone with everything everybody else wants. The best bet is to never stand out in a crowd either too rich or too poor. It may become obvious that you are putting on, and that is no good. In a real, long term survival event, there will be many poor, starving people that are real hobos, so you should fit right in. Learn how a hobo lives. Could you find, prepare, and eat a meal out of a dumpster? You would be surprised how many Americans do every day.

Life Is Precious

I'm not telling you to be a coward or not to protect your possessions. I am suggesting that life, especially yours and mine, will become more precious as more and more people die from the disaster. Losing your life or receiving injuries, because you boasted about having gasoline stored in your outbuilding, is just not worth the risk. If you think you can protect your possessions or your loved ones with firepower, better think again. There is always someone with more firepower. It's far easier to hide your possessions and tell no one about them. Having firepower is fine if you are highly trained and experienced in its use.

Firearms

I know there are people out there who suggest you buy guns, bullets, and gold and silver for the coming fall of society, but unless you are willing to receive proper and regular training and take the time to become and stay highly skilled in the use of any weapon, in my opinion, you are better off leaving them alone. If, on the other hand, you become knowledgeable and proficient in the safe use of firearms and practice often, then firearms will certainly have a place in some situations. Always remember, your best weapon is you mind.

Guns and ammo will become valuable barter items of exchange, but unless you can defend yourself during the trade, what's to keep the other person from shooting you and taking your guns and ammo? If you are planning to barter these types of items or even possess them, you better learn how to use them well and have a real plan to keep them hidden. Protecting firearms and ammo and bartering them will require that you become highly skilled at self-defense & security or have one or more highly trained people helping you.

MAKING A LIVING

A System of Exchange

Let's suppose the disaster I described at the beginning of this guide continues on as a survival event for many years. Let's suppose several scattered groups of people, including you, manage to get together and help each other survive, through bartering, and helping to protect what the group has. At some point, a system of rated exchange may become necessary. Such a system would provide written or stated values for given items of exchange. For example, a can of beef stew might be equal in value to a gallon of drinking water. Some form of bartering auction might be established for valuable or rare items. Rare items would be listed or stated at a higher value than common items. This is similar to how gold is valued against other paper currency in the world markets every day.

Profiting from Gold & Silver

Having a few gold and silver U.S. coins on hand will certainly give you some emotional comfort and may become quite valuable in the early days of an economic collapse. I prefer 1964 and earlier United States Minted Silver 90% coins with dimes and quarters being my personal favorites. However, when water, food, and safe shelter becomes scarce, gold and silver will, in my opinion, become almost worthless. If you can acquire some gold & silver during the event at a very low or no costs, it is possible that they may have some higher value in the future when the disaster event is officially over. It could take a long time. Your best bet in my opinion is US gold coins & US silver coins (1964 and earlier), both 90% precious metals or .999 gold or silver bullion. If you are not absolutely sure what it is, do not buy it. Fakes exist now that are almost impossible to tell unless you are an expert and have the equipment to test the gold and silver. Fakes will become more common during a crisis. Remember, if it is too good to be true, it is!

Trading for A Living

Values can become established only when enough time and equitable trading has passed to know what others are willing to pay in kind and who to trust. Once such a system is established, people can return to some level of working to produce a form of income. Like the Old West doctors who worked for chickens and eggs, if you have chickens and eggs; there's a good chance you may find a doctor who will provide you with medical care in trade for some of those eggs. Knowledge of how to locate and prepare edible wild plants will be a very valuable skill. Having knowledge and experience in living off the land, trapping, hunting, killing, preparing, and eating animals will be of great value. (Check out my survival books at _www.SurviveUntilTheEndComes.com_.) If you are skilled at primitive trap and snare making, as well as how to set them up and make them work, you will do well as a trader. Knowing how to properly make and use primitive weapons will be a valuable skill. Knowing how to find and properly use edible and medicinal plants will be a tradable skill. The making of cordage, weaving, sewing, making cloths, tanning hides, and other such primitive or lost skills will be of great value. Learn how to teach people. If you are skilled at something, find some people and practicing teaching. A person who can learn something quick and teach it to others will have a highly tradable skill during a long term disaster. A person who can secure water, build a fire, purify the water, build a decent shelter, and locate food will be worth their weight in gold (or should I say beef jerky and gasoline), especially if they can teach their skills to others.

Income in Kind

Producing "income in kind" will require that you offer a needed or desired product or service to those you come to trust. They will, in return for your products or services, offer you theirs, and that is lesson number six. Producing income will require you to work, just as it does now, but not for money or a paycheck. You may be able to use the skills you now have to make a living. Once a group is producing and providing for each other, which may take years, the survival event becomes a new way to live life. It would become a period of adaptability. Eventually, everyone would get used to not having television or greenbacks. Trust would be an important part of this system. Breaking trust with each other, such as lying, cheating, and stealing, would probably have severe, maybe fatal consequences.

Looking for Opportunities

There are always people in America looking for the opportunity to make money, and I suppose a survival event is no different. There will be those who see opportunity in disaster. Charging $20.00 for a gallon of gasoline after a hurricane hits a coastal town is not opportunity seeking. That's simply robbery, especially since the normal supply lines are usually restored in a few days. Some call it price-gouging. People pay the $20.00 because of emotions, primarily fear. This should give you a clue if the power goes out for many months or years. Would someone be justified charging $20.00 for a gallon of gasoline when the power has been out for six months and no gasoline is available anywhere else? Of course they would be, but no one would sell it that cheap, and no one would take cash for it since cash will probably be worthless. I doubt gold coins will buy that gallon of gasoline. That gallon of gasoline might run a small generator for several hours, giving you a chance to pump good drinking water up from your underground well. You might be able to swap that gallon of gasoline for ten gallons of drinking water. Now, which is the most valuable to human life, water or gasoline? This is how you will have to learn to think.

Learn to recognize opportunities now! Investment opportunities will arise during a survival event. If someone has a lot of something they don't want, they may offer you a great opportunity. Someone may offer you a truckload of toilet paper for a few gallons of fuel because they need the warehouse space for something else. You just became an investor and a supplier of toilet paper, at least until the supply runs out.

Opportunity arises for the person who has enough self-control to save back a portion of their earnings to buy into opportunities. I have learned that when times are the hardest and people have no extra money to spend, good opportunities occur at very high levels. I can give you plenty of examples. The best is the Great Depression. The years immediately after the stock market crash of 1929 were years full of depression, starvation, and death. Many people lost all they owned. Some estimate over a million died from starvation right here in America during the Depression. Some took their own lives. Times were bad.

I remember my dad and mom talking about the Depression times. They both lived through it. They both told that their families were so poor the Depression didn't really bother them that much. It was people who had great possessions, especially paper possessions such as stocks and bonds that were most devastated. Many people who owed money to banks and couldn't pay the payments lost their businesses, farms, and homes. Large families were put out on the city streets and country back roads of America. People never understood why their friends at the bank would do that to them. The banks had great difficulty selling the properties to recover the loans because no one was buying. No one thought the banks would put them on the street. They did! And they will do it again. They are required to do so, by law. In fact, they are throwing people out on the streets every day. Just look it up on the internet and see how many foreclosures have been issued since 2007. It will boggle the mind.

As I make final edits to this guide in February 2016, our world economy is still in very bad shape. There were over 4.9 million foreclosures in America from the crash in 2008 through January 2014. It's difficult to find accurate data with all the misinformation out there, especially on the internet. Christmas sales in 2015 were apparently terrible. Many large corporate retail businesses are closing stores and laying off thousands of workers. Some in the government tell us everything is great and getting better, but I cannot seem to find any real growth out on the street. Banks are still kicking people right out on the street. Everyone talks about a recovery, so where's it at? Are we in a new form of the Great Depression or is it some form of the creation of a new world order?

The real ironic thing about the Great Depression was that during all those bad times, some of the very best opportunities existed only to those few people who had reserves and the courage to buy into them. Anybody with $100 could have bought name brand company stock for pennies per share. If they could have held onto those stocks for 20 years, they could have become quite wealthy. Land was "dirt cheap" too. I suppose that expression was coined during the Great Depression. Homes couldn't be given away. It was illegal to possess investment gold. In 1929, one-dollar worth of silver was almost equal to the real purchasing power of a printed US dollar which has always been an interesting phenomenon to me.

A few Americans became very wealthy during the years following the Great Depression. People called them opportunists and crooks. Without their investments and risk-taking, there is a good chance America would have become a third-world communist nation by 1935. The industrialists and capitalists, that's right, the people of Wall Street, provided jobs whether we like them or not. Many of those jobs were hard, laborious jobs, but they put food on the table for millions of hungry Americans.

A few of those workers learned how to save and invest their money when opportunity arose, too.

Opportunity seems to present itself at its greatest levels when very few, if any, have the resources or money to acquire it, and that is lesson seven. Can you imagine the opportunities that would exist during a disaster such as the one I described at the beginning of this book? I'm not an opportunist, and I'm not telling you to be one, either. I am suggesting that if we survive, we must learn to live on beyond the event. We must learn to buy and sell things without money, through the art of bartering. We must learn to save and hide things of value so that when things we need become available; we might have the "money in kind" available to buy them. We must learn to recognize real opportunity when it arises and to take advantage of it quickly (lesson eight). We must become traders of goods, services, knowledge and skills (lesson nine).

Justification

Imagine! The disaster has occurred. Millions are dead. You live and are trying to walk back to your home, and along the way you come across a tractor-trailer crashed off an embankment with the contents spilled out everywhere. The driver is dead. No one else has been around the wreck as far as you can tell. The truck was loaded with hundreds of cases of food and other items being distributed to area retail stores. What will you do? Does opportunity present itself in the middle of a terrible situation? Will it be illegal to take a few cases of the food and hide them somewhere? Will it be morally wrong to steal the food? It's not

69

yours, is it?

Will placing a $100 bill in the shirt pocket of the dead driver in payment of the food make you feel better? Or, will you get down on your hands and knees and thank God for such an opportunity? I cannot answer these questions for you. I'm not exactly sure what I would do. I do know that as soon as others find that canned food, it will be taken quickly. Martial law will probably require that you be shot for taking that food and merchandise. What if some of the cases contained camping supplies or over-the-counter medical products? What if you simply carry a few cases away from the wreck scene, cover your tracks on your last trip, and carefully bury them for later use? Once all the other cases are taken by others and the scene forgotten about, you can return and dig yours up. You don't actually steal it; you just hide it from thieves, don't you? Or did you steal it? What if the driver is not dead but in a coma? That changes everything doesn't it? Or does it? We need to think about these things now, before all hell breaks loose. How far would you be willing to go? I don't think anyone could truly answer that question, (including me), until they are plunged deep into the survival event. For now, just think about it.

These are the kind of issues you may find yourself dealing with during a long-term survival situation. If you and your family are starving, those cans of food will be a blessing from God to you. Things will change. Laws will change. People will be forced to change. Those who have, may find others wanting to take it away. We may be tested to the very core of morality. Our belief system, itself, may be tested to the very limits of humanity. That's exactly where the line of reason must be drawn. People have survived group survival situations by becoming cannibals, while others in the group, refusing to be a part of cannibalism, starved to death, and became dinner.

Your Values

When a real disaster occurs, you will have to develop your own rules, or strengthen the ones you already have. When America got into World War II, we lost some early battles. Films were made of Americans being stripped of their clothes, boots, weapons, and any food they may have had. The public outcry was, "These terrible, immoral people stealing from our dead soldiers have to be stopped." The American propaganda machine used such war clips and narration of the enemy's "treacherous deeds" to help get Americans fully behind the war. Those early, tragic losses, made America much stronger to fight the big battles ahead. Most who stole were locals so close to starvation and freezing to death that they did not see anything wrong with taking something from a dead body that they could possibly keep themselves alive with. I doubt that they considered rank or country of origin of the dead person about to provide them with a warm wool coat or a square meal from a box of C-Rations.

I'm sure that there were terrible people who took weapons, ammo, and other goods from all sides of the war to sell in what is often called an underground black market. In fact, it's likely that some made a lot of money picking up guns that were left behind, vehicles, and many other items of war. If they were fortunate enough to find cigarettes or alcohol just laying around you can be sure they were going to take it. When these people break into locked buildings, businesses, pharmacies, and liquor stores to take what they what, it's stealing and it usually called looting and is usually punishable by death. Its likely people somewhere in the world make their living this way, today.

Reason & Rational Thinking

When warring factions pull out of battlefields, it's common to leave things behind. Some of these things are worthless and some quite valuable. You must establish a line of reason. What can you assume? What actions can you take and live with? What about the dead driver of that truck I mentioned before? You have been walking for miles in your city dress shoes. This driver happens to have the exact same size feet as you. This driver has on a new pair of expensive leather hiking boots. Would swapping shoes with this driver be a crime? Would it be a sin, or would it be common sense and totally rational to swap them?

As you get out of the truck with your new shoes on, you notice a .357 magnum pistol in the floorboard of the truck. You look in the glove box, and sure enough there's a full box of cartridges. Where do you draw the line? What if it is below freezing and that dead driver has a nice winter parka in the sleeper, just your size. In reality, you are taking from the dead. In reality, the dead will not be able to use the coat, shoes, or gun, or deliver the food from the trailer to its destination. Morality suggests it's wrong to steal. It's a sin. The same type of thinking could suggest to you that your God has provided food and clothes for you. Almighty God must surely want you to live through this for some important reason. You will have to answer those questions for yourself should the need ever arise. For now, just consider them.

Learn to See

Look for opportunity every day. The more you practice the better you will get. Keep up with what's going on around you and around the world. Stay informed locally, nationally, and internationally. Opportunity will present itself over and over, but only if you recognize it. Some people will call me an opportunist. All people who survive bad situations may learn how to take advantage of every opportunity presented to them. Survivors must keep mistakes and missed opportunities to a minimum and we must learn valuable lessons from the mistakes we make and live through. No, you do not have to harm or be mean to people to take advantage of opportunities. Just learn to recognize when opportunity is knocking on your door. Learn to save for a rainy day. During a long-term survival event, those hidden cases of food and merchandise will be tradable for all kinds of valuables, and maybe keep you from starving.

FINDING EXTRA MONEY NOW

Learning how to make more money now, before disaster strikes, will help you become a better trader as well as provide some funding for your barter and survival supplies. What can you do right now to put money in your pocket? I'm neither a financial advisor nor accountant, but I have learned a few things about money over the years. If you want to put some money in your pocket, stop spending it so fast (lesson ten). You must spend less than you make. Quite simple, isn't it? If you are not making enough, even after cutting back on spending, then you must make more money (lesson eleven). Let me repeat those two. Spend less than you make and make more than you spend!

Keep a Spending Record

In a little book, write down every trip, every mile, and the purpose of the trip. In another section write down everything you eat, the cost, and the approximate calories. Log every penny you spend and for what purpose in another section. Get receipts for everything. It will take a few days to develop the habit of getting receipts and writing it down. If you pay cash, be sure and write these payments down too. Do this for two weeks. Now, look back at the purchases and determine what were really needs and what were not. What was quality needs purchases and what was junk or emotional purchases? Was money wasted? Answer the questions as if you have been starving for two weeks. Keep writing everything down for an additional two weeks. During these two weeks before you buy anything, ask yourself, "Do I really need this? What if I were starving? Would I buy it?" If you don't buy, put the money immediately in your survival fund. Do not avoid doing this! This practice is very important. To become good at bartering you must learn the value of money, what money really is, and the truth about purchasing power. That is lesson twelve.

Cut Back & Add to Your Survival Fund

Make one less trip to the places where you spend money each week. Buy one less bag of junk food. Rent one less movie per week, and eat out one less time per week. If you do that, you will probably end up with quite a bit of extra cash at the end of the week. Start right now with a pad and pen, record every penny you spend, and be accurate. Do this and you will find many ways you can save back some cash without cutting into your savings or retirement, or severely cutting back your lifestyle. You will not need to take out loans, either, to build your survival fund. In fact, I want you to get out of debt! I'll show you how shortly.

Instead of eating a $50.00 meal in a restaurant, have a grilled sandwich at home. If you still feel the need to eat out, go to a place where you can get a square meal for under $10.00. Consider a sub shop or buffet where you don't have to leave tips. Just try it for a week or two. Cut back on frivolous spending or, spending on things you buy, don't really need, and regret buying. If you want a new suit of clothes but know you do not really need it, wait 24 hours before you make the purchase. If after 24 hours you still want that suit of clothes, or shoes, or whatever, then so be it. It will be yours. On the other hand, if after 24 hours, the burning desire for that new shiny suit of clothes, or shiny car, or whatever no longer burns, then you have found some extra cash for your survival fund. Learn to buy items you use, like canned food, when they are on sale and stock up on them. Be sure they have good "use by dates" and be sure it's things you like.

Your Survival Fund

What are you going to do with your survival fund? Buy some of the things I have discussed in this book (and in my books *Survive Until the End Comes* and *Survival Preppers Domesday Survival Checklist* at *www.SurviveUntilTheEndsComes.com*). Maybe you will put together some survival kits or first aid kits. Maybe you will purchase a small generator. Maybe you will put up a shelf with some survival rations and water, and carefully monitor the dates. Maybe you will purchase some things that might be used as money should the need ever arise. Whatever you purchase with your survival cash, remember to purchase things you can always use for yourself before the dates run out or before the items get too old to use. If you purchase batteries for the shelf, just replace them every year with fresh ones and use the old ones in your radio or MP3 player.

How to Cut Back On Smoking

If you smoke cigarettes, try this. If you smoke three packs a day over a 16-hour waking period that's about 3.75 cigarettes per hour or about one cigarette every 15 minutes. Just skip one cigarette per hour. Getting over that one urge per hour is easy. The urge only lasts a few minutes. Cut up a plastic drinking straw into three equal pieces about the length of a cigarette and put them where you keep your smokes. When the urge hits, pull out one of these straws instead of a cigarette and chew on it, draw air through it, and hold it in your fingers just like a cigarette. Just don't light it. In a few minutes, the urge to light up will pass. I know this works. The power of the good Lord and those plastic straws saved me from starting back many times. I smoked six packs a day for years. I quit smoking 'cold turkey' on November 1, 1996. I haven't smoked since. At a typical current cost of 25¢ per cigarette, if you cut out one cigarette per hour, sixteen times per day for 30 days, you will have over $120.00 for your survival fund. In six months of saving this newfound wealth, you will have enough to buy a small portable generator.

Breaking Undesirable Habits

We usually learn and develop habitual behavior over a long time. It will probably take some time to retrain yourself enough to break the habit. Don't despair. You don't have to think about the long term. Just think about now. Just don't smoke for this moment in time. Don't eat that piece of pizza at this moment. You can have it later if you want, but just skip it now. If you drink mixed drinks at a bar, substitute every other drink with a glass of ice water. Ask for some water to be put into the glass you just finished. Drink the water before you order the next drink and take you time. You will save a lot of money. Food is where the real savings are. Study what and how you eat for a while. Do you eat out often? Do you eat out more than three times per week? Do you leave big tips? If you spend over $200.00 per week eating out, then you can find a less expensive place where no tips are required, eat less expensive meals, or learn to cook. You can buy a fresh cut steak and cook it yourself for much less than one ordered at a restaurant. You could easily save $5,200 per year or more by reducing the number of times you eat out and reducing the cost of the meals that you eat out. If you visit the grocery store more than twice a week, you may be spending much more than you could be. Get their sale papers or look them up on the internet. Join their savings card program. When you are at the checkout, ask for a member card and ask if you can fill it out later. Most store employees will let you. Then use the card but never provide them any personal information. If you don't want to bother with this, just ask the person in front or behind if you can use theirs. If that doesn't work, ask the store employee. Sometimes they will have a card laying there just for such an occasion. Its big brother! Just don't give them any personal information about you. You will save money at the grocery store using their card. Most of their sales are only available to club or discount card holders. Write your grocery list based on sale items that you like. Try to stock a few extras of the sale items.

Cutting Auto Costs

I'm going to make this one simple. You have a good car that gets 24 miles per gallon of gas. You drive 20,000 miles per year or an average of 55 miles per day. According to most statistics, that car costs you about 60¢ per mile to own and drive. If you cut just ten miles per day off your driving, you could potentially save about $2,190.00 per year. Looking at fuel consumption only, you will purchase about 834 gallons of gasoline to drive your car 20,000 miles. At $3.00 per gallon that's about $2,500.00 per year in fuel purchases. Cutting back on your driving ten miles per day could potentially save you $500.00 per year in fuel costs; put another way, driving 16,000 miles per year with a car that gets 32 miles per gallon could save you $1,000 per year in fuel alone. Gasoline was recorded approaching $4.00 per gallon in early 2013. Drive a little less and save more for your survival fund. Gas is around $1.80 per gallon currently in early 2016, but it will not stay at that price long. In fact, thinking of opportunities, properly storing a few gallons of 93 octane gasoline with stabilizer at around $2.00 per gallon would be a great short term investment.

Don't Sacrifice – Just Save

There are many things that you can cut back on without sacrificing or suffering, or doing without the things you want. A penny here, a penny there, saved.... and all of a sudden you will have a bunch of dollars available to you for your survival fund. Do you ever leave the lights on when they should have been turned off? Do you ever leave your television on all night or on when no one is watching? Just start turning off things that you are not using and you will start saving. Turn off the water while you are brushing your teeth. Start making 'saving' your habit. Most of what I am talking about will not even require that you sacrifice. If you really want to acquire some almost instant cash, just stop buying things you don't need, and plan for and comparison shop for the things you do need, especially groceries.

Don't Spend Your Survival Fund On Junk

There is one very important point to what I am telling you about cutting back. You must keep or put back the extra money you save from cutting back. If you don't save it, then there is no point in cutting back. Don't spend your newfound wealth. Get out of debt first! Once you are clear of debt, you will have plenty of money to prepare for disasters and tough times when they happen.

Learning to drastically cut back now will help teach you the true value of money and make it easier to do when disaster strikes.

Hold On to Your Money

Learn to hold onto your money a lot longer. The longer you hold onto your survival fund the more care you will use when considering spending some part of it. Put a little money back every time you make some new money. If you get a raise, put a portion of it back from every paycheck. Ideally, you should be saving 10% to 20% of all your income, anyway, according to financial experts. I'm talking about extra money. If you get a $40 per week raise, put $4 into your survival fund. If you sell something for $500, put $50 of it in your survival fund. Before long, you will have enough money to fund your survival supplies as discussed in this book. Don't take out loans or use your savings or retirement for survival funding; just cut back a little every day until your survival fund is complete.

Should you trust banks? Just go online and see what banks are doing to the people of Greece. Should you trust brokers and financial advisers? Consider the thousands of people who lost much of their retirement accounts when the 2008 financial storm hit. Yes, there are some good banks, bankers, brokers, and financial advisers out there. The problem is, they have to do what their company or the government tells them to do. They may think they are doing you a favor putting all of your retirement funds into one or two unknown stocks, that will, sooner or later, become worth much less than when they put you in those unknown stocks. Brokers make money whether you win or lose and they make money on buys and sells. Remember that! Are they really acting in your behalf for your own best interest? Would it be better if you managed your own money? Think about it! There is only one reason to invest in anything. To make money. Not to make money for everybody else, but to make you money. It's your hard earned money. Don't give it up easy.

Funding Your Survival & Barter Needs

How much will it cost to fund your survival needs, and why have a survival fund at all? You do not have to buy one survival supply or barter item, but it makes common sense to at least have good home and auto first aid kits, a basic survival kit, some food and water on hand and a few high value barter items. (Check out my new book, *Survival Preppers Doomsday Survival Checklist* at *www.SurviveUntilTheEndComes.com*.) Having emergency funds available would help if a hurricane was approaching, but as you know, prices go up on the things you may want days before a hurricane hits. It's still better to have a seven-day supply of water and food on hand. Having a few batteries and flashlights will not break you up or take up too much space. Having a three-day supply of military-style MRE's or Meals Ready to Eat will not break you up and they have a shelf life of many years. Having a few candles and a small camp stove on hand for power outages will not cause you to miss many trips to the restaurant. How much? It will not cost you that much to acquire, over time, most of the items discussed in this book. It also depends on how secure having these survival or barter goods on hand will make you feel. You can spend nothing at all; a few hundred dollars, or a few thousand. If you spend it over a year's time, you will probably never miss it. Just don't borrow money or take your family's lifestyle away to fund your survival and barter goods. They will not like you (or me), very much if you cut out the family vacation. Just carry a sandwich to work for a few weeks and you will have most of the money you will need to start a good survival fund. Some survival events may give you a few days to prepare. So having some cash on hand and a little real silver & gold would be a good thing if you have go to the store in the middle of the night; especially if banks declare a bank holiday after the event. Don't wait too long to get started. We may not have long until the paper money becomes worthless. Learning the real value of the money you earn now and what money really is will make you a much better trader when times get hard. Learning to barter and trade now will make you more industrious and put some money in your survival fund. You will become a better communicator and negotiator. You will learn to deal with all types of people under all kinds of circumstances.

DEBT & FINANCIAL HEALTH

In this section I will discuss debt and the dangers of using credit as money to purchase with. The following thoughts I am about to share are for your consideration, only. If you need financial or legal advice, talk to an accountant, lawyer, or other professional advisor. What I present here is from my own experiences and observations. If someone gets behind paying their bills due to reduction of income, it may be considered a hardship by some lenders, and they may provide a reduced payment plan for you. Other lenders may simply want their money and will go to great lengths to get it.

Secure Debt

There are primarily two types of loans with some variations. One is "secured debt" where you borrow money against the value of something, and if you do not pay, the lender can sell it to recover any outstanding balance on the loan. Home loans are secured debt typically called mortgages, and if you do not pay, the process of the lender taking the home back and selling it is called foreclosure. A first mortgage is usually a loan to buy a home or build one from scratch. These loans typically represent up to about 80% of the value of the home. As time goes by and you make your mortgage payments, the value of the home traditionally increases and your amount owed decreases. If you sold the home at market value, you would have some cash left over. This is basically known as "equity". Lenders often make second mortgages on this equity. These loans, also known as home equity loans, added to the balance of the first mortgage often exceed the current market value of the home. The idea is, I suppose, that lending to people who have good jobs, nice homes, and a good repayment history will make consistent payments, and over time the value of the home will rise and the loan amount will drop keeping the lender in a relatively safe position. Most home loans are given based on a professional appraisal that usually considers the estimated value of the home, as well as the selling price of similar homes in the same market area.

Another kind of secured debt is the classic vehicle loan. Most automobile buyers seem to be more concerned with the monthly payment than the total cost of the automobile. Some automobile finance companies will loan 100% of the price of the car with no money down. When buyers fail to make payments, the finance company or lender can repossess or take possession of the automobile and sell it for as much as they can get. What the sale does not cover, they can sue for the difference. New automobiles have a factory suggested selling price. This is usually referred to as the "sticker price" because of the large price label placed in one of the windows. Dealers who sell "payments" rather than automobiles rarely sell much below sticker and usually tag on hundreds of dollars of transfer fees and closing costs. Used automobile dealers have several wholesale and retail pricing guides that give suggested prices based on age, condition, and general market conditions for that year. Some dealers seem to pay little attention to price guides, especially if they have several lenders ready to offer financing to just about anyone, even people with bad credit histories. Since the credit crash of 2008, it has become tougher to buy anything on credit. The government auto buyback program made sure there were no cheap used cars around anymore. Before the buyback program, you could find a decent running high millage car for $500 to $1,000. It would get you by. Not anymore!

Another type of secured debt is when you own marketable securities, such as bank notes or certificates of deposit, and wish to borrow money against their value rather than sell them or cash them out. Some whole life policies also allow holders to make loans against the cash value of their policies. Basically, lenders will loan about 50% of the current market value of quality securities and notes.

Lastly, another type of secured loan is a "pawn shop loan". If you do not make regular payments or pick up the item by a certain date by repaying the loan with interest and fees, the item becomes property of the pawn shop.

Unsecured Debt

The second type of loan is called an "unsecured loan". This includes money you receive on your signature, good credit record, and payment history. Unsecured debt includes credit cards, personal loans, most department store loan programs, and the classic "loan shark" type loans. Many unsecured loans are very high interest and some lenders really get uptight when you miss a payment or two. Some finance companies that hand out money to just about anyone, use collection tactics that border on being illegal, and in some cases may be. True loan sharks will give you just about any amount for a specific amount of time and require almost double the amount back. If you do not pay, you get beat up or killed. These operations are illegal and taking money from them is probably violating some type of law, too.

Credit cards issued by big banks are probably one of the largest forms of unsecured credit. Credit cards are probably the most abused. Most unsecured debt, including credit cards, issue a credit or loan limit based on your credit history and their theories about your ability to pay. In the recent past, some credit card companies issue credit cards to new customers without performing a credit check. Sometimes these banks would give credit limits up to $5,000 without checking your credit. Not anymore. It has all changed since the 2008 credit crash. A 2016 update: Credit card companies and auto financing companies are making it a little easier to obtain credit. Payments and interest are high. In my opinion this is very dangerous for the economy considering it still poor condition.

Economic Recession 101

When the economy weakens, usually, consumer incomes go down and retail prices go up. Recessions cause inflation and job losses. People reduce spending, start cutting back and saving some money. In time, the system corrects itself, especially when governments leave the free market alone to do its own form of cleaning house. Supply and demand rule the recovery. Recessions are bad news for the most of us. It is the worst possible time for the price of food to go up when incomes are declining due to job losses. When you see these signs, get out of debt as fast as possible! Unemployed people who are drawing money haven't really considered what will happen when the money runs out, have they? In August 2015, it is estimated that over 100 million people are out of work. The reason most of them do not show up in unemployment numbers is that they have quit looking for a job. Full-time, high quality jobs are just not out there in high enough numbers to get a real recovery going. Yet, in early 2016 the government is telling us everything is getting better. They tell us unemployment is going down. However, several big retailers have announced store closings and the laying off of thousands of employees and the reduction in hours for other employees.

The really terrible numbers are the underemployed workers.

If you work 30 hours for $10.00 per hour at a fast food restaurant with no insurance and no benefits, you are statistically employed. If you worked in a job in 2006 making $75,000 a year with good insurance and benefits, you were statistically employed. You took a $60,000 cut in pay, and a $30,000 cut in insurance and benefits, lost your home to the bank and live in a rented trailer. How can our government call that employed? They do!

America Is in Trouble

According to 2012 statistics, the US government was borrowing billions of dollars a day and will owe over 21 trillion dollars by the end of 2015. By the end of 2015, most economist indicate that there will be a deficit of over 600 billion dollars. Simply put, our government is spending 600 billion more dollars per year than they take in. In the beginning of 2016 the stock market has taken hard hits almost daily. Oil prices continue to drop due to massive overproduction by oil producing countries, so they tell us. It's very difficult to obtain accurate data. Most numbers people suggest that the deficit is much larger because many expenses are not included in standard budgets. Our tax base seems to be falling and dollars continue to be printed. It doesn't take a mathematical genius to figure out America is in trouble. What will happen to the country when the government is bankrupt and no other country wants to loan us money. Many other countries are almost insolvent, and they are depending on us to bail them out. If a person is deep in debt, has assets, and the economy collapses, you can be sure they will take your assets and put you out on the street, or worse in a special camp for the masses. Millions starved or died during the Great Depression.

Help just didn't come and many of them were thrown out of their homes by banks and the government. Will they do it again? They already are!

When someone gets behind on a debt, the lender starts calling on the phone trying to encourage the borrower to pay up. The lender usually sends a nice letter as a reminder that you are behind on a payment. When you fall behind two or more payments, you can be sure that the calls from the collector will become more frequent and the letters will become more demanding. You may be threatened that you are in default. When someone becomes three payments behind, lenders of secure debt, such as a mortgage or a vehicle loan, may seek to recover their money by foreclosing on the home or repossessing the automobile. In essence, they will claim ownership of the item and sell it to pay off as much of the loan as possible. Usually, the borrower is still responsible for the remainder of the loan that the sale did not cover. There are no hard and fast rules regarding when lenders may demand their money. Their contracts that borrowers sign usually state that the lender may pursue or not pursue certain collection actions. These contracts sometimes give the lender great freedom as to how to collect their money or not even try. It's up to them.

Read The Fine Print

Be careful what you sign. Read it and understand the terms before you agree to some wild one-sided contract. Foreclosures and repossessions sometimes involve certain people that make quite a bit of money off of your financial hard times. For example, a car is repossessed that has $24,500 owed on it. This car would sell on the lot of a reputable dealer for about $19,500 according to book value and basic selling prices. The car is repossessed and sold to some friend of the lender (who happens to be a car dealer), for $9,500. This kind of underhanded practice happens all the time, and although it may be legal to the letter, I suspect that money changes hands under the table. People like that, during a real long-term disaster, will probably either mysteriously disappear or become leaders of groups of thugs.

Don't Trust Money Lenders

Lenders generally study someone's credit report when they get behind on their payments. Lenders probably look at your total payments and try and determine if they are the only ones not receiving their money. I'm not certain, but I think their procedures for collecting may be different for different situations. If they feel (or their computer tells them), that they can collect or that the borrower is worth a lot of money and is just not giving it up, they may sue for full payment. It would be costly and foolish to sue someone that has no money and nothing to sell, but lenders sometimes do just that. Most will try and work with people whose income has dropped. I believe that the overall condition of the economy may have something to do with how lenders try to collect, too. If many borrowers are not paying on time, then lenders may rethink their collection procedures. If the economy is booming, then they may be quicker to seek every method of collection available to them. These, of course, are my opinions.

Working It Out

Some lenders will work out deferred programs by closing your account and extending the length of time you may pay, thus reducing the amount of your monthly payment. Some lenders will refinance your entire loan and work out lower interest rates and longer terms to lower your payment. Some lenders, depending on how unsecure your loan is and how likely they think it is that they will not be repaid any portion of the loan, may offer deep discounts and drastically reduced interest on your loan. Some may offer to take $1,000 or more off the price of the loan and split the remainder in three payments if you agree to pay it off. Some may make other concessions up to half the value of the loan to get you to agree to pay it off. I do not know of any hard and fast rules or published procedures about settlements. I suppose it is totally up to the lender if they wish to offer you any settlement, such as payment reduction, loan reduction, or deferment plan. I think it may depend on how far behind you are on the payments and how your credit report looks to the lender. If your income and expenses seem to indicate that you should be able to pay the payments, they may certainly seek relief by declaring you in default and suing you for the balance. If, on the other hand, your credit report looks like you are a day from bankruptcy and you call wishing to work things out, you might get some help from your lender.

Dealing with Creditors

Remember, I am not an accountant or lawyer. I am just offering my thoughts on the subject from some of my own personal experiences. If you are in trouble with money, seek the help of professionals. I will warn you about companies that offer so-called debt relief. There are a few reputable ones (usually non-profit agencies), and many less reputable ones. If they ask for large amounts of money from you up front, beware! The good ones do not offer the "wiping out of your debt", but rather, negotiate logical payment plans with your creditors. You can do that, yourself, if you have the stamina. Always check out any debt relief organization with the Better Business Bureau and the Federal Trade Commission.

Call your creditors and talk to them about your situation. Make sure the person on the other end notes on your account that you called and are trying to work something out. Have a clear and accurate budget worked out and give yourself plenty of room for error. Leave no bill payment out. People that call you and demand payments are often commissioned salespeople working at a call center totally unattached to the company who loaned you money. Call your creditors directly and ask for a supervisor. Never accept the first person who answers (unless they are a supervisor), and never accept their first offer of settlement, especially on the first call. Be as nice as you can and have all your financials available. They will ask you many questions about your situation. Do not lie to them. Be as accurate as you can, and remain calm if they seem hateful.

If you get someone on the phone that will not listen to you or is being rude, hang up. Call back until you get someone on the phone that you can understand, that is nice, and has the authority to make settlement decisions for their company. Always ask for a supervisor. Remember, they are recording your conversation, so be careful what you promise and say. If you do not understand what they are offering you, tell them clearly you do not understand and ask them to repeat it. Take your time and write down everything promised to you and everything you promise to them. Do not rush the conversation. Be quite and listen. Take notes. You will be put on hold several times and it may take an hour or more on your first call to get an offer.

Learn to Negotiate

Be prepared to negotiate. They may tell you that they must have $465, today, (or whatever amount you are behind), to get you current before they can make any concessions or lower your payment. If you possessed $465, then you would not be behind in the first place. The reason you are calling is to let them know that you do not have the money and are requesting that they help you out. Warning! Do not agree to things you cannot do. They will try and talk you into sending them your house payment to catch up on your credit card payments. Tell them clearly what you can do. Make them an offer only if you can continue to do it month-to-month. If you agree that you can make a $50 payment every month and you don't, you may get sued or be forced into bankruptcy. Be sure you can pay what you offer. This process will also help you develop your negotiating skills. Negotiating is another important step in bartering.

If you cannot do what they are asking you to do tell them clearly and in a very humble manner (do not be arrogant or hateful), that you cannot do that and ask specifically, "Is there anything else you can offer me?" You will be put on hold for a few minutes and will receive a reply. If they offer you nothing that you can live with then, with great sorrow, tell them that you cannot do what they are asking you to do and that you just don't have the money. You are in a real hardship. Tell them that you really hoped they could work something out and thank them and hang up. Wait a full 30 days before you call them back. Ignore all the daily harassment calls trying to get you to answer and make a payment or commitment to pay. You do not want to answer these calls. Wait a full 30 days and call them. They will have a record of your last call and the offers made. Go through the whole negotiation process again. You may have to wait another 30 days before you get a great settlement. It's called aging your account. I should tell you that you should not try any of these techniques if you are not really having a hardship. They can sue you at any time for the balance and you will probably get a bad report on your credit file that will reduce your credit score. You can also hire professionals to do all this for you, but be sure you are dealing with a reputable professional such as an attorney or non-profit organization that specializes in debt relief. They want your money too. Remember that.

Making The Deal

Some credit cards may be using some government help money for these offers they make, and may be under strict regulations about how they make you an offer of reduced payments. You may learn that no offer exists until you have fallen three or more months behind. It may even be six months in some cases. They usually will not tell you either. They can't! This is usually called "aging the account". Once an account is aged for a certain period, then the door may open for some special offers. What I'm telling you may not even be available now, but you can call each card company and try to get them to tell you what is. Ask questions like, "What if I can't get started making payments for at least six months, would there be any help then?" Be nice and keep asking questions. Never accept their first offer, at least not initially. Tell them you have to look at your finances and that you will call them back. Get the extension and name of the person you are dealing with. Call the back exactly as you told them you would and ask if they have any better offers. Explain that the funds are just not available. Keep working with them and be nice. Once they make you an offer you can live with, take it. If you think you cannot make the payment, ask if they can lower it to an amount you think you can pay. They may even write off a portion of your bill. It's called a settlement. You agree to settle for a certain amount to be paid over time usually with low or no interest.

When they make you and offer and agree to it, they may try and require you to have it drawn out of your checking. Most financial professionals do not suggest you give creditors your personal checking or other numbers. Tell them you will mail the check on time every month for the amount you agreed on. If they refuse, clearly state that you are trying to repay your debt and that you're sorry that they will not work with you, thank them, and hang up the phone.

Call back the next day and explain that you want to pay your bills, and ask if the company has your offer to pay recorded on their computer. If they do not, repeat your offer. If they do, ask them why they are not willing to work with someone who is trying to pay them what they are owed. Be nice! You know you aren't keeping your end of the agreement, but the terms have changed.

94

You are not making the money you were making when you agreed to the terms. This is no excuse, and they can sue you, but it may help. Most will work with you to some extent. Don't necessarily accept the first offer they make you. Just keep telling them you do not have the money to pay that much until they, either work it out, or clearly refuse. Talk to a professional about your situation. Many offer to take care of all this for you for a fee, just be sure they are real professionals such as licensed accountants or lawyers.

Get Out Now!

Will this wreck your credit? If someone is in a bad credit situation, their credit is probably already damaged to some degree. Do not worry too much about your credit now. Banks are not even loaning money to good credit risks, now. You should know that if things return to normal, you should be able to pay everything on time and before long you will have more credit than you can repay. Hmm.... maybe this is what caused all the problems in the first place.... too much credit! Could it be good for you to have less credit? If you never seem to be able to repay what you borrow, maybe it would be better if you pay cash for what you buy, at least until you learn how to operate without borrowed money. Maybe it is time for you to get out of debt and stay out of debt.

If you are in trouble financially, it would be good for you to talk to a professional who is experienced in handling people's financial problems, such as a good attorney who specializes in helping you pay off your loans. Some attorneys specialize in bankruptcies, but reputable lawyers would never advise bankruptcy unless the financials suggested it as the only way. I have never been bankrupt, but I know many people who have. Some it seemed to save, and some it seemed to destroy; so study on it, carefully, before you act. Call your creditors. Talk to professional and reputable financial counselors. Talk to reputable lawyers who have helped people in the past that have been in your situation. Get out of debt! Start creating your barter savings account now. If you have assets of value, then getting out of debt, especially secured debt, is vital before the collapse comes. They can take your assets anytime they want.

Walking Away

If you're willing to walk away (easier said than done), and carry some of your survival and barter supplies with you, then start thinking now about how you would do that. Make a plan and practice carrying it out. How will you move your supplies? Should you consider preparing hidden sealed & secure containers of supplies at various locations away from your home? There is a great chapter on bugging out in my comprehensive survival book, *www.SurviveUntilTheEndComes.com*.

PRACTICE LESSONS

To put all this together and make it yours, I have designed some simple practice lessons. Do them! If at first you don't succeed, keep trying until you do. You will succeed at bartering. The more trading you do, the better you will get at it.

(1). Go to a privately owned restaurant and ask if there is some work you can do for a hot meal. Do this! Just swallow your pride, dress middle class (no hobo this time), and tell them you just need a hot meal and you would be willing to wash dishes, sweep, wash windows, whatever. You do not have to explain and you should not lie. If they persist, just explain that you would rather not get into it, but that you are really hungry. Tell them you do not want a handout, just swap some work for food. Go out of town, find a privately owned restaurant and do this. Don't work all day for a meal, but give them much more than their meal would cost. If one restaurant turns you down, try another. If an employee offers to pay for your meal, take it! You have succeeded in negotiating for your meal. Eat and leave, thanking them quietly. Get their name and address and mail them their money, in cash and add $10 for their trouble. Put in a note that simply says, "Thanks for the meal!" The goal in this practice is to learn to clearly and specifically ask for what you need. Clearly tell them what you are willing to do in return for the meal. Don't tell them why you are doing this. You could come up with all kind of wild lies about why you are starving, but absolutely don't! You could try to make them feel sorry for you, but don't. Simply ask if they would swap a meal for some work. Look around. What needs doing? The entrance may need sweeping. The entry door glasses may need cleaning. Trash may need to be hauled out. If the owner is not there, offer to do some work for an employee if they will buy your lunch. Some will come up will all kinds of reasons they can't allow you to do this, but be persistent. Don't give up easy, but don't push it so hard they call the police either. Be nice! In this vital practice you are simply negotiating a simple, but vital swap. You are using no unique or emotional tricks to get them to do this. "I need a hot meal! I do not have any money. What can I do for you to obtain it?" No tricks, no lies, no cons! Work on this until you get a meal. Do a good job for them and thank them when you are finished. Once you have overcome the first negotiation try something a little harder, like swapping your labor for a few gallons of gas. I cannot put into words the tremendous value of this first barter experience. It will help you overcome many fears and you will learn many new experiences from it.

(2). Swap a skill. If you don't have any tradable skills, learn a new one now. If you think about it, you already have plenty of skills to offer. A skill is not washing dishes or hauling out the garbage. A skill is a learned or skilled trade or something most people do not know how to do. Photography, plumbing, carpentry, auto repair, appliance service and maintenance are all skills. Sewing or alterations, selling, writing, proofing, and all forms of teaching are learned skills. Skills are usually measured by the length of study and amount of real-world practical experience the person has. In other words, if you are a surgeon just out of school, you will not be able to command the income of a thirty-year veteran surgeon who spent three years as a battlefield surgeon and twelve years in a large hospital performing multiple surgeries daily. You might laugh, but if you are a surgeon you already know that everybody thinks you are rich and because of that you pay double for everything. Try finding a car tire dealer who needs a wart removed for a set of tires. A doctor or dentist would never have to pay cash again, for anything, if they would think about it. You could swap some of your skills for teeth cleaning or a filling or maybe some high-quality surgical procedures, as needed, of course. You do not have to be a professional such as a doctor or dentist if you are good at something and have some experience at it. Suppose you are skilled at home canning meats and foods from your garden. You could offer to help your neighbor can their garden beans or some beef from the butcher for something they have, that you want. Remember, practice every day. Once you make a few simple trades, it will get easier and its fun.

(3). Find a retail store and pick out something you want. Now find a person, probably not in the store, that you can negotiate a trade for something you have for the item in the store. Once you have the person desiring what you have offered them, get them to go purchase the item from the store and swap with them. The item you are trading will have to be perceived by the person you're trading with to be much more valuable than the item they will purchase for you in the store. Explain to them that you do not have any cash and you really need the item. This is not as difficult as it sounds. Of course, if you are in a high crime section of a big city, you will probably not find any people interested. They may consider you weird and call the police. On the other hand, if you are in a nice community, in the daytime, and negotiate well enough to convince them that you are not a killer, rapist, mugger, or other con, then they might just believe that you do not have any

99

cash and really need the item. This practice will teach you about secondary and multiple person trades as well as convincing people to believe you, so tell the truth. Telling lies to get your trade is not skilled bartering or negotiating, but being a simple con artist. You can do better than that.

(4). Practice working three or more people for different items until you get the item you need or want. Suppose you need a set of tires. You do a little research and learn that the person who does the computer servicing for the auto center needs a new webpage. You happen to be skilled at carpentry. You agree to fix some loose siding on the computer technicians house normally priced at $400, if they will swap their computer services for a set of tires that you specify, listed at $300. You are giving them an advantage of no less than $100 to make it worthwhile for them. They swap computer system virus checks and backups (normally charged to the auto center at $350), for the set of tires. They make you an appointment to have the tires put on and you complete their home repairs. Everyone is happy. These multiple person and item trades can get bogged down in details, but just keep it simple and keep the trades flowing. Don't let anyone think on it too long. If someone is unsure, find someone else to trade with. Once you do a few of these trades, successfully, you will fall in love with them. In the above example, the computer repair person clearly tells the tire dealer what's going on. They are swapping for carpentry work with you who needs the tires. Be sure you get the tires you specified and be sure the quality of all transactions is up to par, or the whole process of barter collapses. If one person in the trading group cheats, then all the deals in that trade sour. Back out and find other people to trade with. Remember, this is practice only for disaster trading. During a disaster, someone who cheats might lose their life. Practice multiple person and item trades often. It will make you a better trader. Problems will arise and you will learn how to solve them and move on.

(5). Start trading bigger items and services. Once you have gained some experience with relative small trades, move on to larger things. Size of the trade is irrelevant. People trade large ticket items such as cars just as easily as small children swap toys. It's the perceived value of each item in the eyes of the trader that matters. If you trade a rare piece of art you own (valued at $100,000), for a small cabin in the mountains (valued at $85,000), and both of you came away happy, then you both have made a good trade. You may not have a $100,000 piece of art, but I bet you have some nice gold jewelry you don't wear any more. When you buy a new or newer car and end up keeping your old car because the dealer just did not want it, try swapping it for something close to the car's value that you really want or need. A swap offer for a car can have a very high perceived value, even above book, especially to someone needing transportation but has little money for purchasing one. Be sure to take care of all the legal paperwork and requirements on these higher ticket trades.

(6). Practice daily! Look around your home and see what you can really part with, especially things you never use. Forget yard sale items and junk. Nobody will trade these things with you except at a yard sale and you will be trading junk for junk. That can be great training for you, working yard sales, but you need to try and find items that have some value above junk. Start with what you perceive to be worth $5.00. Then move on up to more expensive items. Big flea markets, gun shows, trade fairs, and public auctions can all be great places to practice your trading. Be sure to know what rules and regulations are in place at these events and follow them or you may get into trouble. Try to keep cash out of the trade as much as you can. Make the trade equitable where everyone walks away happy.

(7). Start looking for opportunity daily. Look for it locally, regionally, and nationally. When you watch or listen to the world news, try and think about what might become an opportunity from the events that are happening around the world. If you see a local opportunity try and profit from it by bartering into the opportunity. Practice daily and you will become better and better at it.

SUMMARY

Bartering is fun and exciting to learn and practice, especially before a real disaster occurs. You might even profit from it. Practice daily. Getting out of debt will give you freedom you never imagined. Save up for your bartering fund and start purchasing your survival and bartering items now, before times get hard. Use common sense and get started now. The time is closer than you think. Try to make a good trade at least once a week.

To learn more about surviving disasters look me up online at your favorite book seller or go to my webpage _www.SurviveUntilTheEndComes.com_. There you will find links to some great discounts for my other books. Thank you for purchasing this book.

www.ingramcontent.com/pod-product-compliance
Lightning Source LLC
Chambersburg PA
CBHW062040280526
45788CB00003B/1049